HE'S GONNA **TOOT**
AND I'M GONNA **SCOOT**

Other Books by Barbara Johnson

Where Does a Mother Go to Resign?

Fresh Elastic for Stretched-Out Moms

Stick a Geranium in Your Hat and Be Happy!

Splashes of Joy in the Cesspools of Life

*Pack Up Your Gloomees in a Great Big Box,
Then Sit on the Lid and Laugh!*

Mama, Get the Hammer! There's a Fly on Papa's Head!

I'm So Glad You Told Me What I Didn't Wanna Hear

Living Somewhere Between Estrogen and Death

Joy Journal

Boomerang Joy

Children's Books

The Upside-Down Frown and Splashes of Joy

Super-Scrumptious Jelly Donuts Sprinkled with Hugs

BARBARA JOHNSON

Waiting for Gabriel's Horn

WORD PUBLISHING

NASHVILLE

A Thomas Nelson Company

Unless otherwise indicated, Scripture quotations used in this book are from the Holy Bible, New International Version (NIV). Copyright © 1973, 1978, 1984 International Bible Society. Used by permission of Zondervan Bible Publishers. Other Scripture references are from the following sources:

The Holy Bible, New Century Version (NCV), copyright © 1987, 1988, 1991 by Word Publishing, Nashville, Tennessee. Used by permission.

The King James Version of the Bible (KJV).

The New American Standard Bible (NASB), © 1960, 1962, 1963, 1968, 1971, 1972, 1973, 1975, 1977 by the Lockman Foundation. Used by permission.

The New King James Version (NKJV), copyright © 1979, 1980, 1982, 1992, Thomas Nelson, Inc., publisher. Used by permission.

The Living Bible (TLB). Copyright © 1971 by Tyndale House Publishers, Wheaton, Ill. Used by permission.

The New Revised Standard Version of the Bible (NRSV) copyright © 1989 by the Division of Christian Education of the National Council of the Churches of Christ in the United States of America. Used by permission.

The Revised Standard Version of the Bible (RSV), copyright © 1946, 1952, 1971, 1973 by the Division of Christian Education of the National Council of the Churches of Christ in the USA.

Jokes, stories, and quips included in this volume have been contributed by our many friends, and we have diligently tried to identify the material's origin. Where no source is named, the writer is unknown. Please contact the publisher if you can positively identify the source of any unattributed jokes or stories, and proper attribution will be made in future printings.

Library of Congress Cataloging-in-Publication Data
Johnson, Barbara (Barbara E.)
    He's gonna toot and I'm gonna scoot : waiting for Gabriel's horn / by Barbara Johnson.
        p.   cm.
    Includes bibliographical references.
    ISBN 0-8499-3701-9 (trade paper)
    1. Heaven—Christianity. I. Title. II. Title: He is gonna toot and I am gonna scoot.
BT846.2.J64   1999
236'.26—dc21

                                                                                    99-11091
                                                                                    CIP

Printed in the United States of America.
9 0 1 2 3 4 5 6 9 QPV 9 8 7 6 5 4 3 2 1

This book is lovingly dedicated to my good friend Samuel J. Butcher, the talented creator of Precious Moments.

Through his art, his message, and his many creations—especially the beautiful Precious Moments Chapel and the awe-inspiring Fountain of Angels in Carthage, Missouri—Sam shares the gospel with millions from all over the world.

It is such an honor for me to be able to include several of his adorable Precious Moments figures as illustrations. Copying from his original figurines, Sam did the line drawings just for me—and for you, the reader—when we were visiting the Precious Moments Chapel recently. Just as we were leaving, Sam dashed up to us and said he'd been unable to sleep the night before because he was so excited about this project. (We hadn't slept either from all the excitement of being there!) He was so delighted, just like a little child, as he showed us two variations he had drawn in the line drawing of "This World Is Not My Home," shown above. The two additions are things I talk about a lot, but they don't appear on the collectible figurine. Can you find them? (The answer is on page 157.)

Thank you, Sam!

Contents

1. We've Got a One-Way Ticket to Paradise!   1

2. Transposed by Music   23

3. May the Joybells of Heaven Ding-Dong in Your Heart Today   43

4. Stick a Geranium in Your Starry Crown   65

5. Finally, Fabulously Home!   85

6. Angels Watchin' Over Me   109

7. Ain't a Gonna Need This House No Longer   133

Acknowledgments   155

Notes   157

Just a few more weary days and then,
I'll fly away;
To a land where joys shall never end,
I'll fly away.[1]

We've Got a One-Way
Ticket to Paradise!

When Bill and I moved into our California mobile home several years ago, we quickly discovered a potential problem we'd overlooked during our prepurchase visits. As soon as the movers had left and the dust had settled, things gradually became quiet—except for the sound of airplanes flying nearby. We found we were under the approach path for Los Angeles International Airport!

For a day or two, we thought the noise would be a real nuisance, but it wasn't long until we stopped noticing it altogether. And eventually I even came to like this aspect of our neighborhood a few miles east of LAX. As strange as it may sound, I sometimes enjoy standing outside at night and watching the planes approaching at five-mile intervals. Sometimes when I'm able to see the lights of four to six planes, all lined up across the sky from as far as forty miles away, all sorts of heavenly images flood my mind.

In my imagination, those planes aren't just vehicles carrying passengers from Boston or Bangkok; they're not cargo jets hauling oranges to Oakland or pecans to Peoria. Instead, in my mind, the planes are full of joyful Christians, soaring upward, climbing through the night skies, bound for heaven itself.

Sure, it's just my imagination playing games. But isn't that a wonderful image? Just think of the joy those planes would carry if each one was packed with hundreds of heavenbound Christians! That's such a happy picture. It's certainly a contrast to the one that filled my imagination when I first moved to California many years ago. Back then I was so homesick for Michigan, where I grew up, that every time I saw an airplane I imagined it was going home to Michigan—and I wanted to go too! Since then I've met many others who have also longed to go home, wherever that might be—anyplace from Kansas to Korea, Colorado to Cuba.

Now I watch the airplanes flying overhead, and I'm homesick all over again. But it's not Michigan I long for these days. At this stage of my life, I'm homesick for my REAL home—heaven! Standing outside on a moonlit night, imagining those planes flying away to paradise, I have a frozen picture in my mind of all the wonders awaiting us there, and before I know it, I'm almost overwhelmed by the awesome promises of God. (When my neighbors call to ask if I'm all right, I tell them I'm just getting in a little rapture practice!)

A Joyous Preoccupation

Maybe it's just a hormone thing (after all, my last book *was* titled *Living Somewhere Between Estrogen and Death*), but lately, thoughts of heaven have completely absorbed me. It's become such a joyous preoccupation for me that I've collected an amazing assortment of quips, quotes, inspiring stories, motivating ideas, Scripture insights, gospel song lyrics, and funny cartoons about our eternal life in heaven—a collection too good to keep to myself. And the proof that Word Publishing apparently agrees with me is right here in your hands.

This book is intended as a joyful reminder of the wonderful life awaiting us in heaven. In these pages I hope you'll find encouragement (a word that means to *"fill* the heart") as you

"YOU CAN FLY"

Used by permission of Samuel J. Butcher, creator of Precious Moments.

struggle through difficulties, renewal when you find yourself sinking in the spiritual doldrums, and laughter when you think you'll never laugh again. This is a book that, I hope, will reaffirm for every Christian the words to that beautiful chorus:

> I'm going higher, yes, higher some day,
> I'm going higher to stay;
> Over the clouds and beyond the blue sky,
> Going where none ever sicken or die—
> Loved ones to meet in that "Sweet by and by,"
> I'm going higher some day.[2]

And it's a book that should show nonChristians what they're missing. Like someone said, if you want to dwell in the Father's house you have to make your reservation in advance!

Including this introduction, there are seven chapters in this book—because seven is the perfect number, and heaven is perfect. The stories, quotes, and inspiring messages are loosely grouped around my favorite heavenly themes: music, bells, crowns, mansions, angels, and inheritances, along with the "fly away" fun we'll focus on here in chapter 1.

And just like the rest of my books, each chapter ends with a collection of zany jokes and wisecracks, silly poems and touching stories that have made me laugh. As Christians, one of the things we're uniquely qualified to laugh about is death, so I hope you won't mind if we poke a little fun at the Grim Reaper now and then. We're calling the collections "Cloud Busters" because of something I read somewhere. It was an essay that described clouds as "those sorrows . . . which seem to dispute the rule of God."[3] But Jesus "busted" right through that idea when He said we would see Him "coming on the *clouds* of the sky." Another Scripture verse says, "Behold, he cometh with *clouds.*"[4]

Oswald Chambers said that instead of contradicting God's presence, clouds are actually "a sign that He is there." They are "the dust of our Father's feet," he wrote.[5] Now *that's* an image that makes me smile—God kicking up dust as He strides across the skies! And the thought that we'll someday be soaring upward, blasting right through those "dust clouds" on our way to heaven, certainly brings laughter to my heart. Until then, I hope the little gems at the end of each chapter will keep you smiling until your time on earth is finished and you blast off to do some "cloud-busting" of your own!

The Route I'm Hoping For

A friend once closed a letter to me with the quip "Until He comes or until I go!" Given a choice, many of us would agree with Joni Eareckson Tada's eighty-year-old friend who said she was eagerly anticipating heaven but hoped to "stay around for Jesus' return" because, she said, "I never like to miss a good party."[6] Like this woman, most of us probably agree that the BEST way to get to heaven will be if Jesus comes again while we're still alive. Then we can skip death, rendezvous with our Savior in the clouds, and "party" with Him as we enter the gates of heaven. *That's* the route I want to take, just the way the beautiful old hymn describes it:

> Oh, joy! Oh, delight! Should we go without dying,
> No sickness, no sadness, no dread and no crying.
> Caught up through the clouds with our Lord into
>   glory,
> When Jesus receives His own.[7]

This part of Christ's second coming is what biblical scholars call the rapture. The apostle Paul said it will happen like this:

> The Lord himself will come down from heaven, with a loud command, with the voice of the arch-angel and with the trumpet call of God, and the dead in Christ will rise first. After that, we who are still alive and are left will be caught up together with them in the clouds to meet the Lord in the air. And so we will be with the Lord forever.[8]

"JOY TO THE WORLD"

Used by permission of Samuel J. Butcher, creator of Precious Moments.

Or, as we who are a little less sophisticated in spiritual matters put it: *He's gonna toot, and we're gonna scoot!*

A lot of people are saying "toot 'n' scoot" day may not be far off. As one writer suggested, "By every indication which we can gauge, the rapture seems near. Certainly each day that passes brings it twenty-four hours nearer, and each trend that develops points to its coming."[9]

The rapture can't come soon enough for me! I'm ready right now! So if I sometimes seem a little distracted these days, it's not because of advancing age or approaching senility (even though my *next* book will be titled *Living Somewhere*

Between Pampers and Depends). It's because I keep one ear tuned toward heaven, listening for the sound of that trumpet announcing Jesus' return! That's when *I'll* be a soaring cloud buster, myself!

We're Outta Here!

Just think of what that day will be like. Well, actually, it won't be a *day*. First Corinthians 15:52 says it'll happen "in a flash, in the twinkling of an eye." He's gonna blow that trumpet and *poof!* We're outta here!

Someone gave me a darling T-shirt that gives us a glimpse of what this scene may be like. It's a pair of running shoes with little jet trails rising out of them as their Christian owner is zapped up to heaven.

In a Moment...
in the twinkling of an eye. . . .
1 Corinthians 15:52

© Danny Loya

Of course, imagining this scene is one thing—but I don't want to be left here to see it in person! That kind of nightmare

was described in the bestselling novel *Left Behind*. Soon after
the story begins, the rapture occurs, and the people left
behind feel bewildered. The main character is the captain of a
commercial airliner making a transatlantic flight when the
chief flight attendant tells him, "I'm not crazy! See for yourself! All over the plane, people have disappeared."

"It's a joke," he replies. "They're hiding, trying to—"

"WHO'S GONNA FILL YOUR SHOES?"

Used by permission of Samuel J. Butcher, creator of Precious Moments.

"Ray! Their shoes, their socks, their clothes, everything was left behind. These people are *gone!*"[10]

It's true. We won't need our earthly shoes in heaven, where, if the old spiritual hymn is accurate, we'll be walking streets of gold in "dem golden slippers"!

The Shoes of the Sailors

Such thoughts remind me of a trip Bill and I made to Hawaii recently. At Pearl Harbor, we visited the somber memorial to the USS *Arizona,* which sank in 1941 during the surprise attack that pushed America into World War II. The ship now rests on the bottom of the harbor, a sad monument to the 1,177 men who died when it went down.

In my current state of heavenly fixation, the part of the *Arizona*'s story that touched me most poignantly was a detail one of the tour guides shared. He said the contents of the great battleship had been left intact and that divers who visited the ship recently were surprised to find, more than fifty years after the disaster, that the sailors' shoes were still there, right where the brave men had died. Some were under the table where the sailors were playing cards. Others were left beside the bunks where the men were sleeping or by the ship's signal light where they stood watch. Hearing this description, I couldn't help but think that's the way it will be for us when we fly away to heaven.

Someone shared a wonderful story with me about heavenly footwear recently. In the story, a harried woman rushes to a discount store to pick up some last-minute Christmas gifts. The store is packed, the lines are long, and her patience is frayed.

She pushes her piled-high cart into a checkout lane behind two small children. Seeing the little girl's tangled hair and her older brother's shirt with the two buttons missing, the woman wonders where their mother is. The children are almost giddy with excitement as they repeatedly examine the item they are holding: a package containing glittery gold, adult-size, fold-up house slippers.

Finally it's the youngsters' turn to pay, and the boy—he's probably eight or nine—pulls a wad of balled-up dollar bills from his pocket. Carefully he smooths them onto the counter. There are four of them. The clerk rings up their purchase and announces the total: six dollars and thirty-six cents.

The little boy's shoulders sag. Again he digs deep into the pockets of his tattered jeans and pulls out a dime and a penny. There is an awful moment of silence as the little boy looks up at the clerk, perhaps hoping there's been a mistake. "You need two more dollars and two more quarters," she states matter-of-factly.

"Sorry, Lizzie," the little boy says, gently pushing the gold house shoes back across the counter toward the clerk. "We'll have to wait awhile. We gotta save up some more money."

"But Jesus will LOVE these shoes!" wails Lizzie, starting to cry.

The shopper, pushed out of her exhausted numbness by the girl's cry, quickly sizes up the situation and fumbles in her purse. Without a word, she hands three dollar bills to the clerk with a little smile.

"Thank you, lady!" the little boy exclaims.

"Thank you, lady!" the little girl repeats.

"We just *had* to get these shoes for our mama," the boy explains. "She's real sick. Daddy says she's going to heaven soon. He says heaven has streets of gold and Jesus is there. So we wanted to get Mama these shoes. We thought Jesus would smile when He saw 'em on Mama's feet 'cause they'd be like the gold streets."

Imagine yourself and your loved ones walking the streets of gold in matching gold slippers. Won't we be a sight to behold? And if there *are* golden slippers awaiting us in heaven, they sure won't be the discount-store variety!

Filled with Hope for the Sweet By and By

Sad events in our lives here on earth make us long for that day when we'll "meet on that beautiful shore" in the "sweet by and by," as the beautiful old hymn describes heaven. The hope of heaven sustains us in our earthly struggles and pushes us closer to God. As Joni Eareckson Tada said,

Suffering hurries the heart homeward.[11]

For Christians, *home* is *heaven!* That's our eternal home as well as our enduring hope, a hope someone defined as

He
Offers
Peace
Eternal.

The hope of heaven, the knowledge that we'll someday enjoy "peace eternal," means we can face *anything* here on earth as long as we focus on the joy that's waiting for us in heaven. We cling to this hope as a constant reminder in good times and in bad. As the psalmist wrote, "I will *always* have hope."[12]

Today's heavenly forecast:

Reign Forever!!

Have a hope-filled day!

Art by Julie Sawyer, concept by Rosemary Harris. © DaySpring® Cards.

Meet Me at the Pearly Gates

One especially powerful aspect of our heavenly hope is knowing that loved ones who have died are not just "gone" but they've "gone on ahead" to wait for us there. Often this belief is the only thing that can sustain us as we grieve for those we hold dearest. That's something I know from painful experience!

After our son Steve was killed in Vietnam and his things were shipped home to us, we found, in the jacket he had been wearing the day he died, a letter I had written him. It was stained with water from the rice paddy where he had fallen and was black with mold. But the lipstick kiss I'd put on it was still visible. Usually I wrote Steve letters full of jokes or funny tales about his three brothers' latest shenanigans. But something—actually it was Someone—moved me to write a different letter that day. It said:

> Steve, today I felt a special need to reaffirm our faith in eternal life and being prepared to meet God. I particularly wanted to assure you that whether you are at home here in West Covina or over there in Vietnam you are still SAFE in God's hands . . . and even if your life would be sacrificed for us in Vietnam, EVEN THEN, Steve, you are safe in the arms of Jesus. . . .
>
> Somehow today, I wanted to get all this on paper to you to think about . . . and to let you know we are proud and thankful for you, especially for your faith in what we believe also, because it seems to be so important now.
>
> Even death, should it come to us—ANY of us— brings us just a step closer to God and to eternity, because we have placed our faith in Jesus Christ.

What comfort it brought Bill and me to know those thoughts were precious enough to Steve that he defied orders not to carry personal items and tucked that letter into his pocket on the morning he was killed. One of his friends told us later that Steve had shared the letter with him, and he had told Steve, "Man, you gotta keep this one!" And he did.

His death was a terrible loss for us. And so was the death of a second son, Tim, just five years later in a car crash with a drunk driver on his way home from Alaska. In that heart-breaking time, another letter consoled us. It was one Tim had written to a girlfriend describing the wonderful change that had occurred in his life in Alaska. He had recommitted his life to the Lord, he said, and he was eagerly anticipating God's glorious gift of eternal life.

"Time is short," he wrote. A few days later, he was killed.

The only way we survived the deaths of our sons was knowing that both Steve and Tim's final exits here were their grandest entrances there. Now we cherish the knowledge that they're waiting for us just inside the pearly gates—our deposits in heaven. Oh, how eagerly we await that glorious reunion!

Fly Away Home

Holding this rock-solid belief about the glory to come for us and our loved ones not only empowers Christians here on earth to endure tough times, it also inspires us to accomplish great things. For example, songwriter Albert Brumley dreamed of flying away to heaven as he toiled at picking cotton in 1928. The result was Brumley's simple but classic hymn "I'll Fly Away," which opens this chapter.

It's a simple song with a powerful message, and it has been recognized as the "most recorded gospel song in history."[13]

Of course, this idea of flying away to heaven wasn't born in Albert Brumley's mind as he picked cotton anymore than it was an original idea when it landed in my mind as I watched the LAX traffic fly overhead. It's an ancient image described in Scripture:

> The years of our life are three score and ten, yet their span is but toil and trouble; they are soon gone and *we fly away.*[14]

At the end of our lives here on earth, as Christians, our souls "fly away" to heaven. When we think of "R.I.P." carved on a Christian's tombstone, we don't think "rest in peace" but "rejoicing in paradise"!

A touching story reminded me of that promise last year when Swissair Flight 111 crashed off the coast of Nova Scotia. One of the 229 passengers killed in the crash was Jonathan Wilson, a twenty-two-year-old man who was heading for Geneva to work for Youth With a Mission, a ministry that trains young people for outreach mission work around the world. The parting words Jonathan spoke to his family when he left Florida would later take on a double meaning that reminded them he had flown away—not to Europe but to heaven. He told his family he would "be there until the Lord called him home."[15]

This remarkable story proves the point of a little clipping someone sent me recently. To nonbelievers, it's just a joke. To Christians, it's glorious truth.

> When traveling by plane, the Christian said, "If we go down, I go up."

Now we know that young Jonathan—and thousands of other children and moms and dads—are up there, rejoicing along with Steve and Tim. Picturing the happy reunion we'll have someday in that "land beyond the river that we call the sweet forever"[16] brings tears of joy to my eyes. And I like to think that Christian parents and others who've shed so many tears of anguish here on earth may have an even greater capacity for rejoicing up there. As Randy Alcorn said, "All of us will be full of joy in heaven, but some may have more joy because their capacity [has] been stretched through their trust in and obedience to God in this life."[17] How comforting to know the hole left by the loss of our loved ones will be filled in heaven with "joy, joy, joy, joy down in our hearts!"

Whenever this image comes to my mind, such feelings of anticipation sweep over me that I feel like a young child, eagerly awaiting Christmas morning. I can hardly wait!

Toot 'n' Scoot Traffic Goes *Up*

Of course, even though we hope the Lord will return for us soon, there's no way we can know for certain *when* the rapture will occur. So we have to be ready to fly away to heaven at any moment, because, as someone said, the trumpet hasn't sounded yet but the trumpeter is surely warming up!

For that reason (and a few others!) I won't be making reservations with the company in Seattle that's selling tickets for a rocketship ride in the year 2001. The newspaper clipping describing this crazy caper (sent to me by a friend who knows my longing to "fly away" and who suggested this was one way I could do it) says that, on the first day reservations were accepted, fifteen people plopped down a five-thousand-dollar deposit for the three-hour trip, which will ultimately cost each passenger nearly one hundred thousand dollars.[18]

While those daredevils will fly sixty-two miles above the earth, the journey I'm dreaming of will take me much farther than that; I'm heading all the way to eternity! But one thing we'll have in common is that we'll both be headed *up*. (Of course, I won't be coming back *down* like those rocketship passengers!)

While we're not really sure where heaven is, the Bible often refers to it as being *up* or *above*. That produces one of the "side effects" of heavenly thinking. When we're focusing on the joy we'll know in heaven, our thoughts turn heavenward—that's upward. Our hopes rise, and life down here is more bearable.

Recently I saw this story about how a doctor's friends created a touching tribute for him by their upward thinking:

> A doctor who had devoted his life to helping the poor lived over a grocery store in the ghetto of a large city. In front of the grocery store was a sign reading, "Dr. Williams Is Upstairs."
>
> When he died, he had no relatives, and he left no money for his burial. He had never asked for payment from anyone he had ever treated.
>
> The doctor's friends and patients scraped enough

money together to bury the good doctor, but they had no money for a tombstone. It appeared that his grave was going to be unmarked until someone came up with a wonderful suggestion. They took the sign from in front of the grocery store and nailed it to a post over his grave. It made a lovely epitaph: *Dr. Williams Is Upstairs.*[19]

My friends share these little stories with me, knowing how things that touch my heart or make me smile are always welcome in my mailbox. Fortunately, they understand that my sense of humor is a little warped. That's why, after hearing me complain recently that someone's behavior had nearly sent me to the home for the bewildered, a friend sagely remarked:

Barbara, some people are only alive because it's illegal to kill them!

Waiting, Waiting, Waiting . . .

It's true. We have all sorts of problems—and problem people—to contend with while we're waiting for God to take us home. And for people with an impatient temperament, the waiting itself is hard enough to contend with!

We all seem to struggle with impatience. A newspaper article recently reported that the lack of patience has become such a problem that "it wouldn't be surprising if a 12-step program were introduced any day now. Call it IA—Impatience Anonymous."[20] Some folks I know won't even buy frozen dinners if they take longer than five minutes in the microwave!

Here in Southern California, one of the places where we have to do a lot of waiting is in traffic jams. The only good thing about going nowhere on one of our multilane freeways is that it gives me a good excuse to let my mind wander. (Of course, it sometimes wanders off completely, leaving me sitting there wondering where it's wandered to—and wondering where I was going when I got started!)

Here I am, waiting on hold . . .
waiting to speak to a human being . . .
waiting for the Lord to return . . .

I wonder which will happen first?

© Barbara Johnson

Whenever I'm stuck in traffic or forced to do some waiting, I head off on a different path—mental path, that is. My favorite "mind trips" take me right up to heaven. I love thinking about what it will be like when the trumpet toots and we scoot out of here. Even though millions of us will be flying away to meet Jesus in the clouds, isn't it nice to think there will be no traffic jam in the sky, no lines to stand in, and no car problems to contend with? That thought gives us the endurance we need to cling to the *first* part of Psalm 27:14 while enduring the *second* part:

> Be strong and take heart
> and wait for the LORD.

Someone pointed out that we're not the only ones who have to wait. God is also experienced at waiting. When we're struggling through problems here on earth, trying to cope with the trials that block our way home, He longingly waits for us to turn to Him. He watches our stories unfold and waits for us to acknowledge His plan for our lives. He counts our tears and waits for us to cry out to Him. God is there with us wherever we are on the road of life. He is our comfort today as well as our hope for tomorrow. "This is a strange journey we walk," one friend wrote to me, "full of peaks and valleys. But since God is in both places, *we walk unafraid.*"

Frederick Buechner said, "We are as sure to be in trouble as the sparks fly upward, but we will also be 'in Christ.' . . . Ultimately not even sorrow, loss, or death can get at us there."[21] And Billy Graham wrote, "There is no greater joy than the peace and assurance of knowing that, whatever the future may hold, you are secure in the loving arms of the Savior."[22]

What could be better than knowing we're "leaning on the everlasting arms" of Jesus? What could be more encouraging than remembering that we're loved by the almighty One who created us—and died for us! What could be more rewarding than the knowledge that the Carpenter from Nazareth has built mansions for us in heaven! And those inspiring facts are just *part* of the reason why heaven will be so wonderful. The real reason is much simpler. As Charles Dickens wrote:

> You never can think what a good place Heaven is without knowing who He was and what He did.

Dickens's words remind me of the *real* reason why heaven will be so glorious: because in heaven we'll be with Jesus.

> When Christ shall come
> with shout of acclamation
> And take me home,
> what joy shall fill my heart!
>
> Then I shall bow
> in humble adoration
> And there proclaim,
> my God, how great Thou art![23]

Cloud Busters

Frankly, I'm fed *up* with *up*. From the moment I wake *up* in the morning, it seems I'm playing catch-*up* with *up* until I think I'll wind *up* locked *up* in a mental ward.

At straight-*up* seven o'clock, I lock *up* the house, start *up* the car, and hurry *up* to get to the office. At work I'm either looking *up* some facts, speaking *up* at a meeting, or standing *up* for what I believe in. I know it's *up* to me to hold *up* the truth. When my allotted time is *up* and I've finally used *up* every opportunity to stir *up* enthusiasm for my *up*standing position, I give *up* and hope those others aren't mixed *up* about the points I've brought *up* for discussion.

Then I lock *up* the office and head home to brighten *up* my family's evening by stirring *up* something for dinner, knowing they've worked *up* an appetite.

My husband says I'm too worked *up* about *up*. He'd really like me to shut *up* and stop being so *up*set. I'm trying, but every time I give *up*, *up* pops *up* again!

Up is really starting to get me down!

Ann Luna

Always read books that will make you look good if you die in the middle of it.[24]

Epitaph over a dentist's grave:
He is filling his last cavity.[25]

© Bil Keane

Experience is something you don't get until just after you need it.[26]

Bumper Sticker: When you do a good deed, get a receipt—in case heaven is like the IRS.

Bishop Fulton Sheen once went shopping at a department store. He got on an elevator at the fifth floor and pushed the button for the sixth. Before the doors closed, a woman rushed on, and as the elevator rose, she said, "I didn't want to go up. I wanted to go down."

She turned to Bishop Sheen and added, "I didn't think I could go wrong following you."

"Madam," replied the bishop, "I only take people up, not down."[27]

Bumper Sticker: Rapture *Ready!*

Oh, that I had the wings of a dove!
I would fly away and be at rest.[28]

A man had just undergone surgery, and as he came out of the anesthesia, he said, "Why are all the blinds drawn, Doctor?"

"There's a big fire across the street, and we didn't want you to wake up and think the operation was a failure."[29]

"Hey, Annette! Put this on! He should be coming to any minute!"

Under His wings I am safely abiding;
Though the night deepens and tempests are wild,
Still I can trust Him: I know He will keep me;
He has redeemed me and I am His child.

Under His wings, under His wings,
Who from His love can sever?
Under His wings my soul shall abide,
Safely abide forever.[1]

Transposed by Music

It was a scene right out of *I Love Lucy*, that episode where Lucy's working in the chocolate factory, frantically assembling boxes of truffles—and stuffing her mouth full of the "extras" she can't catch before they move on down the assembly line. In one of my first jobs as a teenager I, too, worked on a conveyor belt. But instead of chocolates, I repeatedly braced myself for an avalanche of dimpled, white Walter Hagen golf balls.

When my coworker yelled, "Let 'em roll!" the jaws of a large chute would open wide, emptying hundreds of golf balls onto the fast-moving belt. My job was to scoop up the balls at lightning speed, a dozen at a time, arrange them in boxes like egg crates, and then rotate the balls so that the stamped name of Walter Hagen was on top and would be visible when the carton was opened. The trick was to get all the balls safely inserted into their little carton before the chute opened again and another batch came tumbling down the line.

At first the job was simply stressful. Then it became stressfully boring. Sometimes, standing there waiting for the chute to open, I felt like one of the contestants on the *Gong Show*, ready to be "gong-ed"—or like Mr. Green Jeans on *Captain Kangaroo* when that feisty Bunny Rabbit showered him every day with ping-pong balls. I spent so much time scooping up the dimpled golf balls I dreamed of drowning in a sea of mothballs. And Walter Hagen's name appeared before my eyes so many times, I swore I'd never play golf—and never name a son Walter if I ever had one! It could have been worse, I suppose, if I'd been a dimple counter. A regulation golf ball has 336 dimples!

The only thing that saved my sanity in that place was music, surely a gift from heaven! Being a pastor's daughter who'd been singing "specials" during church services for years, I'd usually focus on gospel songs. Waiting for the golf balls to rain down on me, I'd sing "Showers of Blessings." Standing there beside the conveyor belt, I'd hum "Standing on the Promises." Grabbing the golf balls before they were "lost," I'd sing "Bringing in the Sheaves" and "Rescue the Perishing."

Now, to be honest, gospel songs weren't the only things that came to my mind. Sometimes a tune of popular music would get stuck in my head, and I'd sing it over and over all day long. Unfortunately, the one that seemed to stick most steadfastly was a ridiculous tune that said, "You can have her, I don't want her, she's too fat for me. Yes, she's too fat for me."

Golf ball-grabbing was just one of the "exciting " jobs that music helped me endure. Another job that ranked low in status and high in tedium was my employment at a dry cleaner's, where my assignment was to snip the buttons off clothes that came in for cleaning. Back in those days, dry-cleaning equipment couldn't handle buttons—they would either break or melt during the process. So the buttons had to be snipped off and put into a little envelope stapled to the cleaning tag. Then they were sewn back on the garment after it had been cleaned. Actually, I was glad to be the snipper instead of the stitcher; sewing is not my gift, and I'm great at losing buttons!

Working there, I'd sing, "What can wash away my sin? Nothing but the blood of Jesus!" and "Have Thine Own Way, Lord," especially the beautiful line that says, "Whiter than snow, Lord, wash me just now, while in Thy presence, humbly I bow." Of course, there, too, stupid lyrics sometimes wedged themselves firmly in my mind. The worst ones were:

> Blest be the tie that binds
> This collar to this shirt.
> For underneath this collar
> Is a tiny speck of dirt.

Whether it was gospel hymns or silly tunes, music was the lifesaver ring I clung to as I bobbled along, enduring these dreary jobs. And while my mindless work at golf ball-grabbing and button-snipping was pretty dull, neither of these summer jobs could hold a candle to the job I still consider the lowest of the low: staple-straightening.

RALPH

"OKAY, THINK DEEPLY AND HOLD IT!"

After I acquired some business skills and had another summer vacation from college, I was hired to be the secretary for a hospital administrator. Friends had told me this particular person was a real jerk to work for and had gone through several secretaries who had left his employment in tears. Since I was considered to be versatile, I was to do a monthly hospital newsletter (that's probably where I got the experience for what I *now* do) and keep the administrator from upsetting the doctors on the staff (he was such a perfectionist that he was known to frequently cause problems).

Whatever his problems were, I figured I could certainly tolerate him for one summer. The fact was, I needed a good-paying job so I could return to college in the fall. So on the first day I put on my most business-like dress and arrived early to impress him. Straightening my desk and putting a new ribbon in the IBM Selectric, I was all set to be his secretary.

The day had only been going a few minutes when he called me into his office to explain my duties. He said that since he was new there, too, he wanted to start out by having me arrange his files the way he'd had them organized in a previous hospital. (Later I learned that he had worked in *several* hospitals in the past and had always left on bad terms.)

So my first assignment, which he wanted done immediately, was to take all the previous administrator's files and "correct" the papers that were stapled with the staple going diagonally across the corner. He wanted me to restaple all the papers so that the staple was *parallel* to the top of the page. To be certain that his instructions were followed *exactly*, he gave me several boxes of special staples that had little zigs and zags in them. They weren't smooth like the ones I had always used in the past.

The job seemed a little ridiculous, but since this was my first day and I was eager to get off to a good start, I hurried to follow his instructions. After I had completed the drawerful of files, I proudly took them back so he could check them. He thumbed through them for a minute then pointed to four more big drawers of files that he wanted restapled! What I wanted to do at that point was staple HIM to the wall!

But I was determined to last out the summer, so I did what was requested of me that day and every day, although most of my assignments were similarly ridiculous. It was challenging trying to satisfy such a jerk, but I learned to discipline myself and get the job done. And in the process I learned a lot about myself and how much I could endure. Then, a few months after the summer ended and I'd gone back to college, I learned that the administrator was in another hospital. But this time he hadn't been *hired;* he'd been *committed*—to a mental hospital! Upon hearing the news, I thanked God that I had done my job without a fuss, so I knew it wasn't ME who had put him there! And I was grateful it wasn't a reverse situation—that he hadn't sent *me* to the home for the bewildered!

In that job, too, I tried to fill my head with comforting gospel songs. (But I must admit, a lot of the time the hymns had titles like "Master, the Tempest Is Raging" and "Out of My Bondage.") The thing about that job that makes me laugh today is that when my husband, Bill, a perfectionist himself, hears me talk about it, he doesn't understand why it's funny! It makes perfectly good sense to him that someone would want to fix all those "incorrect" staples!

A Heavenly Gift from God

In good times and bad, music has always been a part of my life flowing through the laughter as well as the trials. To me, it is a gift from God—a bit of heaven He loans to us while we live on earth to help us survive the hard times, to celebrate the good times, and especially to praise Him in a way no other method can match.

Music has been a golden thread woven through the tapestry of my life, bringing joy into the dark areas. Music reminds me that God's enduring love runs throughout my life and into eternity, a symbol of His promise that someday I'll be rejoining my loved ones in heaven to sing praises to our Lord in person. Whenever I hear especially beautiful gospel music, I imagine that I'm hearing a broadcast performance direct from my eternal home where angelic hymns will be the "Muzak" of heaven!

Singing lifts our spirits. It's just plain good for us. Whether we sing with trained voices that bring thundering applause or off-key screeching, by the time our songs of praise reach heaven they're all equally beautiful. That's what I had to keep telling myself a few years ago when the Billy Graham Crusade came to Anaheim, near our home.

The crusade asked for hundreds of volunteers to enlist in the huge choir that would perform during the event. Because I knew choir members were guaranteed good seats, I was eager to participate. But during rehearsals I realized that choir members would have to be at the stadium much earlier than the audience members, and I knew Bill would want us to attend the event together. So I signed him up, too, although he couldn't stay on key if his life depended on it! (I felt sure the Lord would forgive me this one little bit of deception, because I knew He wouldn't want me to face that crusade traffic alone!)

During rehearsals, I "encouraged" Bill to keep quiet and just mouth the words so his lack of singing ability wouldn't be discovered. Everything went according to plan until the night the crusade began. Then, swept up in all the excitement of the event, with tens of thousands of folks all joining in to sing along with the choir, Bill joined in too. There wouldn't have been a thing wrong with his participating except for one little thing: He was carrying a little tape recorder in his shirt pocket so we could enjoy all the music and messages again later on. That meant he recorded himself loudest of all! And let me just say as kindly as I can: It WASN'T something you'd want to hear again!

Bill has taken a lot of kidding about that recording. But he just says it's not his singing that's off key, it's our ears that are out of tune!

Marvelous Music

Just as music has helped me endure monotonous jobs during my life, it has also encouraged and inspired me in other situations over the years. In times of despair, music has provided soothing comfort. In happy times, it has inspired me to even higher realms of joy. In times of loneliness, it has brought abundant comfort. Truly, it is a gift of heaven on earth!

For example, whenever I hear the hymn "Constantly Abiding" my mind immediately fills with a precious memory

"MAKE A JOYFUL NOISE"

that reminds me of a cherished loved one in heaven. As a small child accompanying my dad to his tent-meeting revivals, I would sometimes perform this song for the crowd. My dad would place a chair on the sawdust floor and lift me up on it so the audience could see me, a cute little girl wearing a bright red dress with its sharply pleated skirt, white, lace stockings, black patent leather shoes, and a big bow holding back the bangs of my Buster Brown haircut. Then, as I sang, my dad would stand beside me, beaming proudly. Sometimes we sang his favorite song, "Under His Wings," together. But whether I was performing solo or with him, his arm was always around me, holding me securely as I stood on the chair and belted out the words.

My dad died suddenly when I was twelve, and I was allowed to choose the music for his funeral service, including "Under His Wings" and "Constantly Abiding."

> There's a peace in my heart that the world never gave,
> A peace it cannot take away;
> Tho' the trials of life may surround like a cloud,
> I've a peace that has come there to stay!
> Constantly abiding, Jesus is mine;
> Constantly abiding, rapture divine;
> He never leaves me lonely, whispers, O, so kind:
> "I will never leave thee," Jesus is mine.[2]

Hearing those hymns now triggers a bittersweet memory—a happy period of my life, which ended with an unhappy experience—that now brings incredible comfort. They instantly transport me back more than half a century to one of those tent meetings somewhere; I can smell the sawdust shavings on the floor and, best of all, remember the comfort of my dad's arm holding me secure.

The Music of Heaven

What a powerful gift music is! Even without words, a familiar melody can bring tears to our eyes or a smile to our lips—

sometimes both. As I arrived at the funeral of a friend recently I was shocked to see in the funeral leaflet that one of the songs to be sung was "If You Could See Me Now." Immediately I imagined Kathie Lee Gifford standing at the railing of a Carnival cruise ship, belting out the company's theme song. Instead, the song, by Kim Noblitt, was a beautiful anthem about the glorious life we'll enjoy in heaven. The chorus says:

> If you could see me now,
> I'm walking streets of gold.
> If you could see me now,
> I'm standing tall and whole.
> If you could see me now,
> You'd know I've seen His face.
> If you could see me now,
> You'd know the pain is erased.

Then the song ends by saying,

> You wouldn't want me to ever leave
> this perfect place
> If you could only see me now.[3]

Isn't that fabulous? Those words transported all of us from that sad occasion of saying good-bye to our friend—to envisioning her frolicking through heaven. What a blessing to all of us it was to picture our friend "walking streets of gold" with happiness radiating from her because she had seen God's face! I don't know about the others attending that memorial service, but I left there almost feeling jealous of the one who had died! One of the first things I did after the funeral was to track down that beautiful song and study the lyrics. They thrill me, creating an image in my mind of what our life in heaven will be like. Reading over the words sends my spirits soaring skyward as I eagerly long for my turn to sit at Jesus' feet.

What a Way to Go!
Another thing that thrilled me recently was a story that appeared in our local newspaper describing the unusual death

of a woman in Santa Ana, California. While it's always sad for those of us who are left behind to say good-bye to a friend or loved one, this woman died in a way that many of us would envy.

> Giesela Lenhart was in full rapture as the Celebration Choir at Calvary Church reached the final verse of "Lord, We Lift Your Name on High." A tall woman, eyes closed, her outstretched arms seemed to reach higher than anyone else's in the riser's back row. Her clear, soprano voice rang out, "From the cross to the grave; from the grave to the sky; Lord, I lift your name on high."
>
> The words meant a great deal to Giesela, who had accepted Jesus as her savior Jan. 20, 1989. And who, at forty-one, may have known more than her share of loneliness and heartache.
>
> They were also her last words.
>
> The final notes sung, her arms still upraised, she fell backward off the riser, victim of a massive [fatal] heart attack.[4]

Reading that article, I couldn't help but think, *Wow! What a way to go!* The newspaper quoted one church member who expressed the same idea: "It would have to be . . . every Christian's ideal: to go 'home' while singing praises to God."

In that second, that "twinkling of an eye," this rejoicing Christian woman was transported from singing in an earthly choir with her fellow church members to rejoicing in the great celestial choir of heaven!

Have you ever thought about who's in that choir? Many of us probably imagine it as a vast angelic group. But as cherished as these angels are, consider that this woman, when she arrived in heaven, had experienced something that even the angels may never have known: *redemption!*

There's a beautiful old hymn, often called "The Angel Song," that makes this point. The chorus says:

Holy, holy, is what the angels sing,
And I expect to help them
Make the courts of heaven ring;
But when I sing redemption's story
They will fold their wings,
For angels never felt the joys
That our salvation brings.[5]

"ANGELS WE HAVE HEARD ON HIGH"

Al Smith's book of hymn histories explains how these beautiful lines came to be written by Johnson Oatman and John R. Sweeney: "One day Mr. Oatman and Mr. Sweeney were reading in the book of Revelation the thrilling word picture of a great choir which will assemble in heaven to sing praises and exalt the Lamb that was slain—the Lord Jesus. As they discussed this thrilling event, they realized that this would be a different choir than ever was heard in heaven before. This one was made up of the 'Redeemed' who had washed their garments white in the blood of the Lamb and, of course, angels couldn't be in this particular choir for they had never experienced the thrill . . . that comes into the heart and life through salvation."[6]

While we may envy the angels already enjoying the wonders of paradise, imagine that they may envy *us* the experience of salvation they can never know themselves! Can't you just picture them gathering around Giesela and saying, "Oooh! Tell us again about the day you were saved! We wanna hear all the details!"

Inspiring Hymns, Glimpses of Heaven
There have been many times in my life when I've wished God would just take me home to heaven right then and there. And what better way to go than in the midst of singing a glorious song of praise to Him? Such wishes often come in times of trouble. And I've had plenty of *that* in my life—my husband's devastating car crash, the death of two sons, and another son's eleven-year estrangement from us.

Sometimes it seemed unbearable. Those of you who have read my other books may remember my telling about a day when I decided to take things into my own hands and drive off a viaduct in an attempt to "fly away" to heaven on my own. But at the last moment I said the prayer of relinquishment—"Whatever, Lord!"—and turned the car around.

Since then I've said, "Whatever, Lord!" many times, knowing that God's plan for me is perfect. But I've also asked for help in living it out—and one of the helps God has given me is the beautiful music of heaven. From the ancient songs of the psalmist and the classic hymns of the Reformation to the modern ballads and praise music of the nineties, gospel music gives us a glimpse of the wonderful life that awaits us in heaven. Just think of all the beautiful songs that provide a preview of paradise:

"I've Got a Home in Gloryland That Outshines the Sun"
"Soon and Very Soon"
"Ivory Palaces"
"We Shall Wear a Crown"
"Lord, Build My Mansion"
"Finally Home"
"It Will Be Glory for Me"

A Funny Thing Happened

A cousin, a witty 85, asked a friend to handle her funeral arrangements and explained she wanted only women pallbearers.

"Why only *women* pallbearers?" the gentleman asked.

"Because," she replied, "men don't take me out now, so why should I let them take me out then?"

—Taylor Reese, author of *HUMOR Is Where You Find It*
Illustration reprinted with permission of *Christian Single* magazine.

Sometimes I join in singing one of these songs, and I'm moved to tears by the images the beautiful words create in my mind. At other times, the stories behind the hymns, like Al Smith's story about "The Angel Song," are as beautiful as the lyrics themselves. In another story about a beautiful hymn, Kenneth Osbeck tells how the third verse of the inspiring song "The Love of God" came to be: "The unusual third stanza . . . was a small part of an ancient lengthy poem composed in 1096 by a Jewish songwriter, Rabbi Mayer, in Worms, Germany. . . . The lines were found one day in revised form on the walls of a patient's room in an insane asylum after the patient's death. The opinion has since been that the unknown patient, during times of sanity, adapted from the Jewish poem what is now the third verse of 'The Love of God.'"[7]

Just imagine this person centuries ago having a mind so tortured that he was imprisoned in an "insane asylum." Yet at times the darkness apparently lifted so that the anguished person became an artist, painstakingly scratching with some unknown instrument these inspiring words into the cold, hard walls:

> Could we with ink the ocean fill
> And were the skies of parchment made,
> Were every stalk on earth a quill
> And every man a scribe by trade
> To write the love of God above
> Would drain the ocean dry,
> Nor could the scroll contain the whole
> Tho' stretched from sky to sky.

The timeless message of this song validates Martin Luther's comment about the power of music. "Next to theology no art is equal to music," he said, "for it is the only one, except theology, which is able to give a quiet and happy mind."[8]

Another Al Smith story tells the equally touching history of that familiar hymn "When the Roll Is Called Up Yonder." It began one day in the late 1800s when James M. Black of

"LET HEAVEN AND NATURE SING"

Williamsport, Pennsylvania, impulsively cut through an alley to save time on his way to the post office. As he hurriedly walked down the alley, he passed "a young girl sweeping the porch of a ramshackled house. She was dressed oh, so poorly, and in her young face were already the traces of worry and neglect," wrote Smith.

Black asked the girl, whose name was Bessie, if she went to Sunday school.

"No, sir," the girl replied. "I'd like to but I don't have anything fit to wear; but sir, how I'd love to go!"

Black and his wife and friends promptly brought the girl

some "church clothes," and she began faithfully attending both Sunday school and another church group called the Epworth League. "Each time there was a roll call, she was there to respond," Smith wrote.

Then came the day when Black called the roll and Bessie failed to answer. Black looked up from the attendance book, surprised. He called her name again, but she was not there. After the service he hurried to the alley, worried that Bessie's drunken father had forbidden her to come or that he had beaten her so severely she was unable to make her way to church. Instead, he found her dying of pneumonia. He summoned his own doctor to treat her, but all efforts failed to save her.

Black couldn't shake off the feeling he'd first experienced when he called the roll and Bessie didn't answer. He thought about how there would be "a roll call in heaven and oh, the sadness there would be for those whose names are not written in the Lamb's Book of Life," Smith wrote. A songleader, Black longed for a song that would "impress this truth upon the hearts" of the young people in his Sunday school class. But he couldn't find one. Later that day he was inspired to write one himself.

"I went into the house and sat down at the piano. Without any effort at all the words seemed to tumble from my mind. . . . The tune then came in the same manner. I felt that I was only the transcriber—I dared not change a note or word," he would explain later.

The song was first sung at Bessie's funeral after Black explained the circumstances leading up to it. "Never will I forget the effect it had upon the large audience of friends who had come. The Lord had taken little Bessie home, but in her place He had given a song to keep reminding all of us to be ready for that great roll-call day."

When the trumpet of the Lord shall sound,
And time shall be no more,
And the morning breaks, eternal, bright and fair;

When the saved of earth shall gather over on the
  other shore,
And the roll is called up yonder, I'll be there.[9]

Cloud Busters

Theme Songs for Biblical Characters

Noah: "Raindrops Keep Falling on My Head"
Adam and Eve: "Strangers in Paradise"
Lazarus: "The Second Time Around"
Esther: "I Feel Pretty"
Job: "I've Got a Right to Sing the Blues"
Moses: "The Happy Wanderer"
Jezebel: "The Lady Is a Tramp"
Samson: "Hair"
Salome: "I Could Have Danced All Night"
Daniel: "The Lions Sleep Tonight"
Joshua: "Good Vibrations"
Peter: "I'm Sorry"
Esau: "Born to Be Wild"
Jeremiah: "Take This Job and Shove It"
Shadrach, Meshach, and Abednego: "Great Balls of Fire!"
The Three Kings: "When You Wish Upon a Star"
Jonah: "Got a Whale of a Tale"
Elijah: "Up, Up, and Away"
Methuselah: "Stayin' Alive"
Moses: "There's a Place for Us"
Nebuchadnezzar: "Crazy"

The trouble with doing something right the first
time is that nobody appreciates how difficult it was.

Laughingstock: Cattle with a sense of humor.

I don't suffer from insanity.
I enjoy every minute of it.

A Hymn for Every Calling

The dentist's hymn: "Crown Him with Many Crowns"
The contractor's hymn: "The Church's One Foundation"
The politician's hymn: "Standing on the Promises"
The boxer's hymn: "Fight the Good Fight"
The meteorologist's hymn: "There Shall Be Showers of
 Blessings"
The IRS's hymn: "All to Thee"
The gossip's hymn: "O for a Thousand Tongues"
The electrician's hymn: "Send the Light"
The baker's hymn: "I Need Thee Every Hour"
The telephone operator's hymn: "We've a Story to Tell to
 the Nations"
The airline captain's hymn: "Jesus, Savior, Pilot Me"
The dieter's hymn: "And Can It Be That I Should Gain?"
The UFO's hymn: "Come, O Thou Traveler Unknown"[10]

A person without a sense of humor is like a wagon
without springs—jolted by every pebble in the road.

Henry Ward Beecher

A woman taught the tiny tots in her Sunday school
class to sing her favorite hymn, "Oh, the Consecrated
Cross I Bear." Then came the Sunday morning when

a concerned mother questioned the teacher about the songs she was teaching the children. Her child told her she'd learned to sing, "Oh, the constipated, cross-eyed bear."[11]

Musical bloopers in church bulletins:

• The pastor will preach his farewell message, after which the choir will sing, "Break Forth into Joy."

• The concert held in Fellowship Hall was a great success. Special thanks are due to the minister's daughter, Gladys, who labored the whole evening at the piano, which, as usual, fell upon her.

• Twenty-two members were present at the church meeting held at the home of Mrs. Marsha Crutchfield last evening. Mrs. Crutchfield and Mrs. Rankin sang a duet, "The Lord Knows Why."[12]

Let the sea resound, and all that is in it; let the fields be jubilant, and everything in them! Then the trees of the forest will sing, they will sing for joy before the LORD, for he comes to judge the earth.[13]

Ring the bells of heaven!
There is joy today,
For a soul, returning from the wild!
See! the Father meets him out upon the way,
Welcoming His weary, wandering child.

Glory! glory! how the angels sing;
Glory! glory! how the loud harps ring!
'Tis the ransomed army, like a mighty sea,
Pealing forth the anthem of the free.[1]

May the Joybells of Heaven
Ding-Dong in Your Heart Today

There's no biblical basis for the cherished image a friend planted in my mind recently when she merrily ended her letter, "May the joybells of heaven ding-dong forever in your heart." There's no mention of heavenly "joybells" in the Bible—no mention of regular bells in heaven, for that matter. The King James Version only mentions the word *bells* three times: twice in telling the Hebrews how to decorate the holy garment Aaron was to wear when he ministered to them as priest and once in Zechariah's prophecy about the inscription that would appear "upon the bells of the horses."²

Still, since bells have always been associated with worship services, we just naturally assume they will be among the many wonderful sounds we will hear when we arrive at the pearly gates. William O. Cushing's beautiful song lyrics, quoted in part on the opposite page, paint a glowing picture of heaven's bells pealing out as a sinner returns "from the wild." The image was made even more powerful for me when I read that Cushing, a powerful preacher during the 1800s, wrote the lyrics after he was forced to leave the pulpit because he "lost his power of speech."

Anguished by his disability, Cushing asked God for another way to serve Him. His prayer was answered when he discovered he had a gift for writing beautiful song lyrics. One of those songs was the thrilling hymn "Ring the Bells of Heaven." Others include "Under His Wings" and "When He Cometh."[3]

The Heavenly Sound of Church Bells

To me there's no more inspiring sound on earth than the heavenly *bonging* of the majestic bells that echo through the streets of small towns and cities everywhere, calling worshipers to church. And there's no more joyous noise than the cacophony of a tower full of church bells clanging away at the end of a worship service as the church doors are thrown open and Christians are released back into the world to spread the good news.

Someone told me about attending a holiday church service late on Christmas Eve in a beautiful old church in the midst of a large city's tall buildings and office towers. When the Christmas Eve service ended just after midnight the churchgoers emerged through the old wooden doors to find snowflakes swirling through the air and the heart of the usually bustling city extraordinarily quiet. Suddenly the church's bells pealed out through the darkness, filling the empty streets with the glad tidings of Christmas, their joyful sounds echoing off the neighboring structures of concrete and steel. It was, my friend said, a most extraordinary moment, one she doesn't expect to equal until she hears those joybells of heaven pealing out a welcome to her.

A recent newspaper story described another woman who'll be listening for the sound of joybells when she arrives in heaven. The article reported a multimillion-dollar donation to the Salvation Army from Joan Kroc, widow of Ray Kroc, who founded the McDonald's fast-food empire. In presenting her gift, Mrs. Kroc described how her billionaire husband "used to dress up as Santa Claus during the holidays and ring the bell for Salvation Army donations on the streets of San Diego. 'Right now, I bet there's a lot of bell ringing going on up there with Ray leading the chorus,'" Mrs. Kroc said.[4]

Maybe I love stories about bells so much because, frankly, I can identify with them. Bells can't help but be joyful, even when some people might not think it's appropriate. They just ring their hearts out, their uplifting tones merrily filling the air even when the situation would seem to call for a more restrained and dignified attitude. That's me!

For example, at Christians' funerals, I'm always *dinging* when everyone else is definitely in the *dong* mode. The normal funeral attire is somber black, but I like to wear bright green.

"RING THOSE CHRISTMAS BELLS"

Used by permission of Samuel J. Butcher, creator of Precious Moments.

You see, green is the color of new life, and while we who are left behind are mourning our loved ones' death, they are more alive than ever, dancing to the music of those glorious joybells in heaven! They are living proof of one of my favorite insights:

Death is not extinguishing the light.
It is turning down the lamp because the dawn has come.

Feeling this way, during mournful memorial services I generate a lot of raised eyebrows and feel a lot of elbows tapping against my ribs—the kind of jabs that silently say, *Stifle yourself, Barb! Don't you know death is serious business?* And I do mourn when a friend dies—but I mourn selfishly, feeling sorry for myself, knowing how I'll miss that person's friendship and wishing that I, too, could be strolling heaven's streets of gold with our beloved Savior.

Reminders of Heaven

At such times I feel a little like the church bells of London during the funeral procession for Princess Diana in 1997. The princess was loved all around the world, and we all mourned her death. Billy Graham noted that Princess Diana "set a wonderful example for all of us by her concern for the poor, the oppressed, the hurting and the sick." But he also noted another thing that her tragic death unintentionally gave us: a reminder "of how fragile life is, and how we should be ready to enter eternity and meet God at any moment."

In all the publicity surrounding Diana's death, one little sentence from a newspaper report has stayed with me longest and caused me to feel sympathy for those majestic London bells. The article said the bells' clappers were wrapped in heavy leather during the funeral procession lest their tones would sound too joyful.

When I read that description, I also couldn't help but think of the contrast between the bells' dull, somber *thuds* during Diana's funeral and the deliriously happy clamor of joybells we expect to hear in heaven. There will be no stifling of their happy sound inside those pearly gates! And if the beautiful old hymn is correct, the voices of angels will "swell the glad triumphant strain." It could be deafening—except there won't be any deafness there. Imagining the glory of it all sends my mind soaring heavenward—and wishing I could settle there *soon*.

Sharing Heaven's Glory

There are many stories about believers who, as they exit this life, manage to share with those they leave behind the joyful noise they hear as they're welcomed into glory. As they step through death's door and enter the portals of heaven, the ecstasy of the welcoming choruses they hear is obvious in the last earthly expressions that pass over their faces—expressions of awe and wonder.

In her book *Mourning Song*, my friend Joyce Landorf Heatherley shared someone's story about professional caregivers and even parents who avoid getting emotionally involved with a "bound-to-die child." As a result the children "die alone because adults deny death for fear of the hurt they might experience after the child has died." In contrast the story describes a mother "who was willing to put down her denial, pick up her own acceptance, and then beautifully prepare her little son for his death."

> She came every day to the hospital to visit her little five-year-old son who was dying of the painful disease lung cancer.
>
> One morning, before the mother got there, a nurse heard the little boy saying, "I hear the bells! I hear the bells! They're ringing!" Over and over that morning nurses and staff heard him.
>
> When the mother arrived she asked one of the nurses how her son had been that day, and the nurse replied, "Oh, he's hallucinating today—it's probably the medication, but he's not making any sense. He keeps on saying he hears bells."

Then that beautiful mother's face came alive with understanding, and she ... said, "You listen to me. He is *not* hallucinating, and he's not out of his head because of any medicine. I told him weeks ago that when the pain in his chest got bad and it was hard to breathe, it meant he was going to leave us. It meant he was going to go to heaven—and that when the pain got *really* bad he was to look up into the corner of his room—towards heaven—and listen for the bells of heaven—*because they'd be ringing for him.*" With that, she [hurried] down that hall, swept into her little son's room, swooped him out of his bed, and rocked him in her arms until the sounds of ringing bells were only quiet echoes, and he was gone.[5]

The mother had prepared her little son for death by helping him look forward to the happiness that awaited him. Perhaps without knowing it, she had followed the advice another author shares with parents:

Telling your children about life and death begins with teaching them the wonderful truths about heaven found in God's Word. Your goal is to fill their hearts with the hope promised by Jesus in the Gospels. The night before His own death, Jesus told His disciples not to let their hearts be troubled, because He was going to prepare a place for them in heaven (John 14:1–4).[6]

That's good advice, not just for children, but for all of us! We can face death with hope when we focus on the thrilling happiness that awaits us, including the joy of seeing our loved ones again. Imagining the young children who are gleefully frolicking in heaven's playground as they await the arrival of their godly parents reminds me of one of Sam Butcher's beautiful Precious Moments porcelain figures. Part

FAMILY CIRCUS

"Heaven is a great big hug that lasts forever."

© Bil Keane

of the "Hallelujah Square" mural in the Precious Moments Chapel, it depicts an adorable little girl arriving at heaven's gate, a tear sliding down her cheek. The comforting angel who greets her is pointing to a bucket labeled "Old Hankies."

Sam titled the scene "No Tears Past the Gate," and whenever I see it, I find myself wiping away tears of joy, just thinking of that marvelous place where Bill and I will be with our sons again and there will *never* be any more tears! What a thought!

A friend wrote a beautiful poem that describes my work with Spatula Ministries and all the ups and downs Bill and I have been through. The last two lines are my favorites. They say:

But when Gabriel blows his trumpet . . . and when Toot
    and Scoot is here,
Barb will jump the gate and grab her boys as Jesus
    dries her tears.

"NO TEARS PAST THE GATE"

That image is so precious to me, I've wallpapered it to my heart. Can't you just see me vaulting over that gate to get to Tim and Steve? Can you imagine the joy I'll know when I hold them in my arms again? (You probably can if you have deposits in heaven, yourself!) And then imagine the Savior joining us in our boisterous reunion, wiping away our tears of joy. Maybe, like Sam Butcher's little angel greeter, He'll remind us of one of the major benefits of our new home. He may point to a sign posted on the pearly gates, sort of like those restaurant signs that say, "No shirt, no shoes, no service." But the heavenly version would say:

> No troubles,
> No trials—
> No tears!

No Honking in Heaven
Yes, if there are bells in heaven, they will surely be joybells, and they'll ring out a glad welcome for our arrival there. Just imagine the difference in the sounds we'll hear as we breathe out our last earthly breath and the next moment draw in the sweet fragrance of heaven. One moment our earthly ears could be filled with the horrific noise of honking horns, screeching brakes, inflating airbags, and ambulance sirens— and the next moment we could be hearing the angelic choir sing music so beautiful it's beyond our comprehension here on earth.

One moment we could be surrounded by the poignant sounds of friends and family members weeping—and the next moment be the focus of exuberant rejoicing at the gates of heaven by loved ones who are waiting for us there.

One moment we could be irritated by the life-ending sounds of an IV alarm beeping, a heart monitor wailing out a "flat line," and a ventilator blasting out an emergency signal—and the next moment hear the blessed voice of the Savior saying, "You're home now, My child. Let Me show you the mansion I've prepared for you."

"I would have been here sooner, but I got hooked on oat bran muffins."

© 1999 Barbara Johnson

We know the sounds of heaven will be, well, *heavenly!* In our celestial home we won't be honked at, yelled at, beeped at, or bonged. We won't have to put up with the irritations of overeager smoke alarms (the signal at my house that dinner is ready), dental drills, jackhammers, barking dogs, or emergency exits left ajar.

When I think of all the noises, big and small, that clutter our days on earth, I'm amazed that we can get anything done at all—and I long for the soothing peacefulness of paradise. Our lives here sometimes seem to be completely controlled by various bells, beeps, and buzzers. For many of us, the day starts when the alarm clock awakens us. We stumble into the bathroom, where the latest invention is a battery-powered toothbrush with a timer that beeps when we've brushed the ideal two minutes. Next we head for the kitchen, where something gets shoved into the microwave. When the bell beeps, breakfast is done.

Some of us push a bunch of beeping buttons to arm a home security system before we go flying out the door. Others of us may have to beep another system to open our car doors. And once we're behind the steering wheel, another bell, beep, or buzzer reminds us to buckle our seat belts. (I'm holding out for one that reminds us to bring along the grocery list, too, and maybe check to make sure our shoes match.) Some cars beep when we put them in reverse (in case we can't tell which direction we're going, I guess); others have bells that chime when we leave the turn signal on too long without turning (which seems silly, because if it's been that long and we still haven't turned we've obviously forgotten where we wanted to turn in the first place, so what good does it do to remind us when we're two miles down the road?).

The modern world is full of emergency alarms, trouble signals, and warning bells. With all these gadgets reminding us to heed the warnings, how on earth do we get ourselves in so much trouble? Quite simply, for one reason or another, we ignore the signals. Or we don't hear them. Or we think they're meant for someone else.

Rise-Up Time

If only we would heed *all* warnings God sends our way! But too often in our busy lifestyles, we're so distracted by our myriad responsibilities that we don't hear the still, small voice that sounds urgent messages in our hearts. Even when we try to set aside time to study His timeless advice we speed on through His Word just like we zip past flashing lights and caution signals in our cars, sure we can squeak by one more time.

God uses all sorts of ways to get our attention, but sometimes we ignore Him, just as we've learned to disregard so many of the modern warning gizmos that have become routine in our high-tech world. When I think of the low-tech, wind-up alarm clocks that were all we had for so many years, I'm amazed at how things have changed. Those old rattletraps broke through the quiet morning sounds of nature with nothing more than a wind-up key that caused a mallet to hammer away at a couple of clanging bells on top of the clock.

For many years, Bill and I used that kind of trusty old alarm clock to start our day. Ironically, now that we've reached retirement age and no longer have jobs we must hurry to each morning, we wake up earlier than ever—usually around 4:30! We don't use an alarm clock at all unless we're traveling in another time zone and have appointments to keep.

Now that I don't *have* to get up at the crack of dawn, I enjoy doing just that. Those early morning hours are precious to me; they may be the closest thing to heaven I experience all day. The phone doesn't ring. There are no loud cars passing by on the street. No letter carriers or UPS deliverers are ringing the doorbell. The day's crises have not yet managed to intrude.

When someone sent me a list of early-risers in the Bible, I was cheered by the thought that the time of day I love so much has always been a special time for God's children. Now while I enjoy those quiet hours of the dawn, I think of my godly predecessors who worked and worshiped before the day began—without any kind of alarm clock to wake them up:

- Abraham got up early and "returned to the place where he had stood before the LORD."

- Moses and Aaron told the Israelites, "In the morning you will see the glory of the LORD."

- Moses climbed Mount Sinai early in the morning to meet God.

- In his last words, King David said a righteous leader who "rules in the fear of God . . . is like the light of morning at sunrise on a cloudless morning."

- Job's "regular custom" was to worship God "early in the morning."

- The psalmist wrote, "In the morning, O LORD, you hear my voice; in the morning I lay my requests before you and wait in expectation."

- Isaiah said, "In the morning my spirit longs for you."[7]

Jesus, Himself, used the early morning hours to communicate with God. The Bible says, "Very early in the morning, while it was still dark, Jesus got up, left the house and went off to a solitary place, where he prayed." And later we're told, "All the people came early in the morning to hear [Jesus] at the temple."[8]

How do you suppose the people managed to wake up early on those days when there were no clanging bells of alarm clocks to jar them loose from their slumber? Surely their excitement about hearing the Savior's words helped them spring up from their beds and hurry to the place where Jesus was speaking.

The Best Sound in Heaven

While heaven's joybells will certainly be wonderful to my ears, the heavenly sound I anticipate most eagerly is that one: Jesus speaking to me, the sound of the Savior calling my name. Can there be anything more blessed in all eternity? That image explains why I consider the events of the resurrection morning one of the most beautiful stories in the Bible.

A distraught Mary Magdalene sobbed outside the empty tomb on that early morning. She had gone there to care for the corpse, and now she was in such anguish, believing someone had stolen Jesus' body, that when the gardener asked her what was wrong she couldn't even turn to look at him as she answered. "They have taken my Lord away," she said, "and I don't know where they have put him."

Then the gardener spoke to her—just one word, her name: "Mary"—and her head jerked up at the sound of his voice. Her spirits soared as she realized he wasn't the gardener at all but Jesus Himself! Imagine the joy that swept through her heart and thrilled her soul to hear that sound: *her name*, coming from the lips of the risen Savior! That's the glorious sound that will awaken us to life eternal when we fall asleep on earth and open our eyes in heaven.

The late Peter Marshall, former chaplain of the U.S. Senate, told a story about a young boy who was dying from an incurable disease. He asked his mother, "What is it like to die? Does it hurt?"

His mother reminded him of what it was like when he had played hard all day and fell asleep on the sofa or in the car on

FAMILY CIRCUS

© Bil Keane

the ride home from his grandparents' house. "When you awoke
in the morning you were in your own bed because your daddy
came with his big strong arms and carried you home. Death is
like that," the mother told him. "You fall asleep here, and you
wake up and find that your Father has carried you home."[9]

The Mysterious Call

Until we wake up in heaven on "that great gettin'-up morning" to the sound of the Savior calling our names, we have to
make the best of the mornings we wake up here on earth. For
millions of people, that means being awakened by the jan-
gling bell, beep, or buzzer of an alarm clock. And yes, there's
a whole new generation of sounds to wake us up these days.
Actually these modern alarms have distanced themselves so
far from the good, old-fashioned, two-clanger alarm clock
that they do everything but ring. Now you can buy clocks
that awaken you with music, recordings, flashing lights, or,
ironically, those same sounds of nature that for centuries have
lulled people to sleep: ocean surf, wind sighing through the
willows, frogs in the forest, creeks gurgling—and all sorts of
other sounds. And not only that, but there are new alarms
that *bing, bong,* and *beep* at us all day long.

I think of them as annoyance noises, those pesky reminders
to take the clothes out of the dryer, fill the car's gas tank, and
stand back so the lettuce can be sprayed with water in the
grocery store's produce aisle.

My own home is full of these noisy gizmos. Friends give
them to me for my Joy Room, and to be honest, it gets so crazy
in there sometimes that I have to go outside and listen to the
freeway to find a "piece of quiet." It seems that something is
always ringing, dinging, or donging.

Recently I announced a moratorium on noisy doodads—
just as Bill brought home yet another silly gift for me: an elec-
tric wind chime! "Look!" he said proudly, pointing to the
wording on the box. "It chimes all by itself, so you can keep it
INSIDE the house. You just plug it in."

Great! I thought, smiling through gritted teeth. *Now all we need is seventy-six trombones and a parade, and we can have round-the-clock mayhem!*

Each new noisemaker provides a splash of humor—at least the first few times we hear it. My friend Lynda gave me an alarm that made some kind of barnyard noise every time I opened the refrigerator. The idea was to keep me from getting into the ice cream so often. But, being a martyr, I selflessly gave the little loudmouth gadget to a friend who needed it more than I did! (And so that I could eat my ice cream in peace!)

Another friend had a different kind of alarm on one of her kitchen appliances. An intelligent, poised, retired schoolteacher, this woman—I'll call her Clara—was watching *Jeopardy!* one night when a crowing sound suddenly reverberated through the house: "Cock-a-doodle-DOOOOOOOO!"

Clara, absorbed in matching wits with the *Jeopardy!* contestants, was startled but couldn't find anything out of the ordinary in the house. She didn't hear the crowing again, so she assumed it was something on the television and settled back for the double-jeopardy segment. The next night, just as *Jeopardy!* was ending, the loud sound came again: "Cock-a-doodle-DOOOOOOOO!"

This time Clara was sure it hadn't come from the television. In fact, the crowing seemed to have come from the kitchen. But when she stood in the middle of the kitchen floor, perplexed, nothing seemed amiss.

The invisible rooster continued every night at exactly the same time, and eventually Clara figured out that it was the new microwave that was crowing. When she told me about it, I insisted on calling her at the appointed time to hear it for myself. Sure enough, at 7:45 P.M. she held the phone up to the microwave, and it crowed loudly: "Cock-a-doodle-DOOOOOOOO!"

By now, Clara's microwave had become quite a sensation among her friends and relatives. One of their favorite things to do was to come over and watch *Jeopardy!* and wait for the microwave to crow. She wrote to the manufacturer, asking if the crowing was a special feature that wasn't described in the owner's manual. The company responded by asking her to send the microwave back to them so they could determine whether a prankster at the factory had somehow programmed the microwave's components with this crowing. But by that time Clara had gotten rather attached to the feisty little rooster living inside the appliance. She decided to keep it as it was.

Eventually the excitement subsided, and Clara and the crowing microwave settled into a comfortable routine. Every night at 7:45, right in the middle of *Jeopardy!*, the microwave cock-a-doodle-DOOOOOOOOOOOO-ed and Clara sighed and smiled, enjoying the cheerful greeting of the mysterious little bird. She had stopped trying to solve the mystery and instead claimed the verse from Proverbs, "It is the glory of God to conceal a matter" and those wise words from Deuteronomy, "The secret things belong to the LORD."[10]

Then one day when her grandson came over to paint her kitchen, he pulled the microwave away from the wall—and found a little round magnet stuck to the back of the appliance. There was a small talking alarm clock attached to the magnet, a gadget used by blind people. Like many such tools for the sight-impaired, instead of buzzing or beeping it crowed like a rooster.

Eventually Clara learned that the little magnet had been given out to those who had contributed to a local support group. She knew her husband had been a faithful supporter of the Society for the Prevention of Blindness, so she assumed the little magnet had been given to him before he died. How it got stuck to the microwave, we'll never know. Perhaps he left it in the cabinet and somehow it fell down the back wall when the new microwave was installed. However it happened, it added a spark to her life while it hid there, crowing away at 7:45 every night. Friends asked about the little bird whenever they called, as though it were a member of the family.

Now the mystery is solved—and *Jeopardy!* doesn't seem nearly as appealing to my friend. She might be the ideal candidate to try that new-fangled microwave described recently in the newspaper. The door doubles as a television and computer. So while the pizza is spinning around inside the oven she could shut the door and log on to the Internet, send an e-mail message, or even watch her favorite television show—*Jeopardy!* It probably wouldn't be as spirit-lifting as a *crowing* microwave, but it could run a close second!

Heavenly Bell-Ringers

We enjoy such stories because they make us laugh (especially when they're about someone else!), but at the same time it's reassuring to think that none of us will be embarrassed by false assumptions and silly scenarios in heaven. We won't be outwitted by crowing gizmos and stumped by mysteries. We'll surely be laughing in heaven—but we'll laugh for the sheer joy of being in the presence of God and our loved ones and all the other members of the heavenly host. As one century-old tombstone in London's Brompton Cemetery so simply but beautifully puts it, we'll be

WITH CHRIST, WHICH IS FAR BETTER.[11]

The sounds that perplex us on earth will be a thing of the past when we walk down those streets of gold. There won't be any irate drivers honking at us. No talking alarm clocks crowing at us. No computers beeping at some mistake we've made. No metal detectors ringing to stop us as we hurry to our offices or airplanes. We'll leave behind all the earthly sounds that frustrated us, as well as all those words that annoyed us. Never again will we hear:

- "Your appointment was yesterday."
- "This lane is closed."
- "Your application is denied."
- "Your account is overdrawn."
- "Your payment is overdue."

- "There's been an accident."
- "The principal wants to see you."
- "We've done all we can do."
- "I'm sorry."
- "Too late."
- "Too bad."
- "Good-bye."
- "Oops!"

Isn't it wonderful to think we're bound for glory, where there will only be joyful sounds and loving words? In that great choir gathered in Hallelujah Square we'll sing what Christians have predicted for decades in the majestic old hymns:

- "We'll sing and shout the victory."
- "Glory in the highest I will shout and sing."
- "Songs of praises I will ever give to Thee."
- "I'll sing with the glittering crown on my brow."
- "And there proclaim, my God, how great Thou art!"

I'm ready right now!

Cloud Busters

I never lay my head upon the pillow without thinking that maybe before the morning breaks the final morning will have dawned. I never begin my work in the morning without thinking that perhaps He may interrupt my work and begin His own. A person with that attitude is surely looking for the Lord's return. It's the only way to live!

G. Campbell Morgan

Days are scrolls:
Write on them only what you want remembered.

Bachya ibn Pakuda

There's nothing discreditable in dying. I've known the most respectable people to do it.

C. S. Lewis,
Letters to an American Lady

The youngest children enrolled in a church preschool always steal the show at the annual Christmas program. Last year the children—none of whom could yet read—held up brightly colored three-foot-high placards that spelled out Christmas words. The highlight came when one foursome walked onstage in reverse order and proudly spelled

RATS

Emergency operator: 911, what is your emergency?
Caller: Could you send the police to my house?
Operator: What's wrong there?
Caller: I called and someone answered the phone, but I'm not there.

It was one of Mother's hectic days. Her small son, who had been playing outside, came in with his pants torn. "You go right in, remove those pants, and start mending them yourself," she ordered.

Sometime later she went to see how he was getting along. The torn pants were lying across the chair, and the door to the cellar, usually kept closed, was open. She called down the stairs loudly and sternly:

"Young man, are you running around down there without your pants on?"

"No, ma'am," was the deep-voiced reply. "I'm just down here reading your gas meter."[12]

Don't you hear those bells now ringing?
Don't you hear the angels singing?
'Tis the glory hallelujah jubilee.
In that far-off sweet forever
Just beyond the shining river,
When they ring the golden bells for you and me.[13]

Hear, O my people, and I will warn you—if you would but listen to me . . . ![14]

I am thinking today of that beautiful land
I shall reach when the sun goeth down;
When thro' wonderful grace by my Savior I stand,
Will there be any stars in my crown?

Will there be any stars, any stars in my crown
When at evening the sun goeth down?
When I wake with the blest in the mansions of rest,
Will there be any stars in my crown?[1]

Stick a Geranium
in Your Starry Crown

It's not unusual for women to tell me that my book *Stick a Geranium in Your Hat and Be Happy* has helped them learn to laugh again during the most miserable days of their lives. The book describes my own journey through the tunnel leading out of the cesspools of life. Most importantly, it shares the relief I found when I learned how God uses humor to hammer out our hurts. When we learn to laugh again despite our difficulties, we live out the premise that "pain is inevitable but misery is optional."

Since the book was published a few years ago, I've met thousands of folks, mostly women, who adopted the "geranium" philosophy and chose to laugh in the midst of heartache. And occasionally I hear about men who have benefited from the book too—usually pastors or Christian counselors. But as far as I know, Duward Campbell was the first cowboy. A tall, tough West Texas rancher, Duward stuck a geranium in his Stetson and looked for every opportunity to laugh in spite of life's difficulties. With a smile on his face and a heart spilling over with God's love, he literally danced his way to death's door.

Soon after he was diagnosed with terminal cancer, someone gave Duward a copy of *Geranium*, and he took it to heart. Even now his wife, Gwen, chuckles when she remembers Duward with a geranium stuck in the band of his cowboy hat as he rode his horse or sipped coffee with his fellow ranchers at the local Dairy Queen.

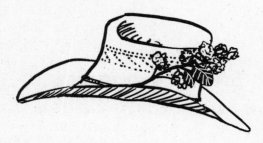

And when Duward became a "geranium cowboy," he didn't just *wear* geraniums; he *raised* them. The flower beds around the Campbells' home in Haskell, Texas, became his geranium project and soon were spilling over with the bright red blossoms. To him, the geraniums weren't just flowers. They were reminders to all who knew him that Duward Campbell, a strong Christian, had consciously decided to laugh instead of complain about his problems. You see, even though he didn't talk about it much, Duward knew he was homeward bound, and that calm assurance gave him the courage to be happy even as he looked death in the face.

My friend Marilyn Meberg often talks about inspiring people "who manage to add to others' cheer by how they exit from life." When someone clipped Duward Campbell's long, glowing obituary from the newspaper and sent it to me, I knew he was one of those people. The eulogy said, in part:

> Cowboy tall at 6'2" and with rugged good looks, Duward was a commanding presence in his community. Even amidst the ravages of cancer, his

indomitable spirit prevailed. Often he stuck a single geranium atop his cowboy hat and quoted the title of Barbara Johnson's book, *So Stick a Geranium in Your Hat and Be Happy*. . . . To his wealth of friends and family, he leaves a legacy of positive thinking, neighborly action and pervasive love.

Just as those red geraniums brightened Duward Campbell's life, he brightened the lives of others—especially his wife and their family, including their beloved grandchildren. He told them about the cancer, the doctor's prediction, and his own decision, despite the bad news, to be happy. And he told them matter-of-factly in his West Texas twang, "You can make up your mind: You can be miserable—you can just lie down and die—or you can stick a geranium in your hat and be happy."

It was obvious to all who knew him which choice Duward had made. He had learned the secret the apostle Paul talked about when he said:

I have learned the secret of being content in any and every situation. . . . I can do everything through him who gives me strength.[2]

Like thousands of joyful Christians who have gone on to heaven before him, Duward Campbell laughed at death. He wasn't afraid to die. And in the fearless way he departed this life, he also inspired the loved ones he left behind.

One of the many happy memories that continue to encourage Gwen is remembering his determination to keep doing the things he enjoyed. One of them was dancing; they had enjoyed many a night doing the Texas Two-Step and the Cotton-Eyed Joe. Gwen laughs now when she remembers how, just a couple of weeks before he died, the two of them were out on the dance floor again, dragging Duward's oxygen tank along behind them as they swirled around the room.

Another bittersweet memory, ironically, is of the day when a Fort Worth doctor told them Duward's cancer had worsened.

"THIS TOO SHALL PASS"

Used by permission of Samuel J. Butcher, creator of Precious Moments.

When the oncologist came in with the results of the latest biopsy, his face was grim. "I'm afraid I have bad news," he began.

"Well, shoot," Duward answered impatiently. "I didn't need you to tell me that. I knew it wasn't good—all my geraniums are dyin'!"

Hearing him say that and fearing that his resolute joy might be weakening, Gwen slipped away and called one of their daughters back in their little hometown. "I don't know how you're going to do it, Honey," she said, "but you girls need to find your daddy some geraniums."

It was late fall, long past the first frost, and as Gwen and Duward made the four-hour drive home from Fort Worth late that evening, Gwen's mind raced ahead, hoping her daughters could find a few geraniums somewhere that were still blooming. As late in the day as she had called and as late in the season as it was, she wasn't sure they'd be able to find even one.

"But when we got home and opened the door," she recalled later, laughing at the memory, "there must have been a million of 'em. The house was full of geraniums."

Duward died in October 1997, and just as they'd filled his home with geraniums when he needed encouragement, his family and friends filled the church with geraniums for his funeral. The floral blanket on his casket was made of geraniums entwined with his cattle-herding rope, and laughter was entwined throughout the service, just as he had requested. When it was over, one of his favorite songs, "Waltz Across Texas," played as his friends paid their last respects.

Recently Gwen Campbell's little grandson, remembering his grandfather's last days, asked her, "Grannie, is PaPa in bed up in heaven?"

"Oh, no, Honey," Gwen said with a smile. "I'm sure he's not in bed. He's not sick anymore."

The grandson's face broke into a smile as he exclaimed, "Grannie, I'll bet he's teachin' Jesus how to do the Cotton-Eyed Joe!"

Getting Used to Wearing a Crown

It's silly, I know. But when I think of Duward Campbell and all the other merry Christians in heaven, dancing on those streets of gold, I imagine them wearing, not the majestic crowns described so beautifully in Scripture, but cowboy hats, baseball caps, firefighter helmets, sunbonnets, and all manner of head coverings—symbols of the work they did on earth. And of course when my imagination is really running wild, I see geranium blossoms bobbing on all the brims!

Some of us just don't seem sophisticated enough to wear heavenly crowns, but that's what the Bible says we'll have—"a crown that will last forever."[3] Here are some of my favorite promises of the crowns that will be available to us in heaven:

I have fought the good fight, I have finished the race, I have kept the faith. Now there is in store for me the crown of righteousness, which the Lord, the righteous Judge, will award to me on that day—and not only to me, but also to all who have longed for his appearing.[4]

Blessed is the man who perseveres under trial, because when he has stood the test, he will receive the crown of life that God has promised to those who love him.[5]

And when the Chief Shepherd appears, you will receive the crown of glory that will never fade away.[6]

For what is our hope, or joy, or crown of rejoicing? Is it not even you in the presence of our Lord Jesus Christ at His coming?[7]

Do you not know that in a race all the runners run, but only one gets the prize? Run in such a way as to get the prize. Everyone who competes in the games goes into strict training. They do it to get a crown that will not last; but we do it to get a crown that will last forever.[8]

A few years ago when Florence Littauer and I were both speaking at a women's conference, I was enthralled by her description of these five kinds of crowns: the crowns of righteousness, of life, of glory, and of rejoicing, and the imperishable crown. She told the audience she'd been a Christian fifteen years before she learned that crowns would be available to her in heaven. "That pepped up my whole Christian life," she quipped, explaining that she'd "always wanted to be a queen."

Florence said her study of the Bible had made her believe that we don't work our way to heaven, but through our work here on earth, some of us may earn these heavenly crowns.

For example, it may be that 2 Timothy 4:8 is telling us the crown of righteousness can be earned by being faithful throughout our Christian life and constantly looking forward to Jesus' second coming. Joni Eareckson Tada says this crown is "for those who are itching to have Jesus come back."

The crown of life may go to those who love God more than themselves and who don't just endure adversity but who rise above it, who show joy in the midst of trials. The old saying is true: There will be no crown-wearers in heaven who were not cross-bearers here on earth!

The crown of glory may be reserved for those who "humble [themselves] under the mighty hand of God" and who "feed [His] lambs" or support those who do.[9]

The crown of rejoicing may be waiting for Christians who share the gospel with others wherever they go.

Finally, the imperishable crown, said Florence, is waiting for those who are disciplined and well-trained in the Christian life. These are the believers who are devoted to prayer and faithful in their Bible study.

Royalty in Training

Now, for some of us, this idea of wearing a crown is going to take some getting used to. It's hard to imagine ourselves with the regal bearing of royalty. Maybe we need a little practice!

In my mind, one of the ways we can prepare ourselves for this royal duty is by setting a good example for our fellow earth-dwellers the way Jesus, our heavenly King of kings, sets an example for us. We know He reigns in love, extending grace to all His subjects. He thinks of us as His children, His sheep, and He nurtures us as we follow His pathway.

In the same way, we prepare ourselves to take our place beside His throne in heaven by practicing love here on earth. We set an example of Christian faith by enduring life's difficulties with courage and even joy, the way Duward Campbell and so many other devoted believers have shown us. And wherever we go, we spread God's care for His children so we can be a conduit of His love to others.

The King of creation wants us, His subjects, to be joyful and to love one another. In fact He has told us that His number-one priority is love: His love for us, our love for Him and for others. So our assignment as heavenly royalty-in-training here on earth is, above all, to spread His love.

Joy Begets Joy

Jesus also wants us to be joyful. But just as some of us have to accustom ourselves to the idea of wearing a heavenly crown, others have to *work* at being joyful until it becomes a habit. Do you know the difference between *joy* and *happiness?* Happiness depends on what is happening around us. But true joy just bubbles up from inside and is constant regardless of our circumstances.

One way to develop the joyful habit is to nurture an attitude of thankfulness. As someone said, God has two dwelling places—one in heaven and the other in a thankful heart. When God dwells in our thankful hearts we can't be anything but joyful. Science confirms that truth. After years of studying people with joyful temperaments, one researcher concluded, "The first secret is gratitude. All happy people are grateful. Ungrateful people cannot be happy."[10]

It's impossible to feel miserable while imagining ourselves wearing the crown Jesus has promised us and saying, "Thank You, God!" It's just as hard to stick a perky geranium in your hat (or your helmet or your ten-gallon Stetson) and be gloomy. If you're not as bold as Duward Campbell was to do it literally, you can at least do it in your imagination. Just envision yourself, no matter what your circumstances, joyfully adorned with a silly hat, or a heavenly crown—as you head out into the world each day. And let your first words of the morning be, "Thank You, God!"

Henri Nouwen offered some additional suggestions for being gratefully joyful. He wrote:

> It might be a good idea to ask ourselves how we develop our capacity to choose for joy. Maybe we

could spend a moment at the end of each day and decide to remember that day—whatever may have happened—as a day to be grateful for. In so doing we increase our heart's capacity to choose joy. And as our hearts become more joyful, we will become, without any special effort, a source of joy for others. Just as sadness begets sadness, so joy begets joy.[11]

RALPH

"THE TESTS ARE BACK, YOUR HIGHNESS, AND I KNOW WHAT'S CAUSING YOUR HEADACHES!"

A Spirit That Gravitates Toward the Light

When your heart is filled with God's love and your head is aglow with His crown, you can't help but express joy. And others invariably "catch" your joyful attitude because, as

Nouwen says, "Joy is contagious." He learned this from a friend who "radiates joy, not because his life is easy, but because he habitually recognizes God's presence in the midst of human suffering, his own as well as others." Nouwen's description of his friend creates a pattern we should all try to copy:

> Wherever he goes, whomever he meets, he is able to see and hear something beautiful, something for which to be grateful. He doesn't deny the great sorrow that surrounds him nor is he blind or deaf to the agonizing sights and sounds of his fellow human beings, but his spirit gravitates toward the light in the darkness and the prayers in the midst of the cries of despair.
>
> His eyes are gentle; his voice is soft. There is nothing sentimental about him. He is a realist, but his deep faith allows him to know that hope is more real than despair, faith more real than distrust, and love more real than fear. It is this spiritual realism that makes him such a joyful man.[12]

The more he was with this joyful friend, said Nouwen, "the more I [caught] glimpses of the sun shining through the clouds. . . . While my friend always spoke about the sun, I kept speaking about the clouds, until one day I realized that it was the sun that allowed me to see the clouds. Those who keep speaking about the sun while walking under a cloudy sky are messengers of hope, the true saints of our day."[13] By "catching" his friend's joy, Nouwen must have also learned the truth Helen Keller taught: "The best and most beautiful things in the world cannot be seen or even touched. They must be felt with the heart."

Crowns Aglow with Stars

We are children of God, members of Jesus' royal family—our Father's light shining through the clouds of others' sorrow. Pop

May the God of hope fill you with all joy and peace as you trust in Him, so that you may overflow with hope by the power of the Holy Spirit. (Romans 15:13)

your imaginary (for now) crown on your head, unleash your brightest smile, and go spread some joy!

Have you ever noticed how one person with a bright smile can light up a room full of sourpusses? Think of the woman described as a "wondrous sign" near the end of Revelation, who was "clothed with the sun, with the moon under her feet and a crown of twelve stars on her head."[14] Just imagining the light given off by such an image makes me want to reach for my sunglasses! But that's the kind of impact we can have as we bring God's Word to those still struggling through their own cesspool.

Empowered by this image, we can walk confidently through life's darkest night. As Norman Vincent Peale often reminded his listeners, we're "not supposed to crawl through life on [our] hands and knees," with our faces in the mud.[15] Let your light shine! Deliberately choose to look for joy in every step of your journey through life and to share it with others. When you do, you will be blessed with happiness no matter what your circumstances are. Remember what Jesus told us to do: "Let your light shine before men, that they may see your good deeds and praise your Father in heaven."[16]

Just as one little pinch of salt can make all the difference in cooking, the light of one joyful Christian can radiate the love of Almighty God to the world. That reminds me of the story about the rich man who called his three sons to his bedside as he was dying. He told them, "I want to leave my fortune intact, so I will set each of you the same task to see which one is the most capable at managing money. In my warehouse there are three large storerooms, all of the same size. Here is a bag of silver each. Your task is this: Each of you fill one storeroom with as much as your silver will buy."

The first son thought long and hard about how he could get the most bulk for his money. He used his silver to buy sand. But even though his money could buy several wagonloads, when the silver ran out, the storeroom was only one-third full.

The second son spent all his silver on plain soil, but it filled only half of his storeroom.

The third son watched his brothers try unsuccessfully to fill their storerooms with the silver their father had given them. Then he spent just a few silver coins and bought some candles and matches . . . to fill his room with light.[17]

The Beginning of Prayer

Someone said a smile is the lighting system of the face and the heating system of the heart. And smiles can easily evolve into laughter, that sound only God's children can make. As Reinhold Niebuhr said,

> Humor is the prelude to faith,
> and laughter is the beginning of prayer.

At first glance, it might be puzzling to think of laughter as the "beginning of prayer." But remember that a happy heart springs from a grateful spirit. Each time you enjoy a hearty laugh see how natural it feels at that moment to chuckle out the beginner's prayer: "Thank You, Lord!"

Brighten the Corner Where You Are

There are so many ways we can wear Christ's light-giving, star-bedecked crown in this world, helping others see God's goodness shining through the clouds. Sometimes it just takes a moment to make a big impact on someone's life.

For example, there's this story about Dr. Albert Schweitzer, the famous missionary-doctor and Nobel Prize winner who spent his life helping "the poorest of the poor" in Africa:

> Reporters and officials gathered at the Chicago railroad station to await the arrival of the Nobel Prize winner.
>
> He stepped off the train—a giant of a man, six-feet-four, with bushy hair and a large mustache.
>
> As cameras flashed, the officials came up with hands outstretched and began telling him how honored they were to meet him. He thanked them and

then, looking over their heads, asked if he might be excused for a moment. He walked through the crowd with quick steps until he reached an elderly woman who was having trouble trying to carry two large suitcases.

He picked up the bags in his big hands and, smiling, escorted the woman to a bus. As he helped her aboard, he wished her a safe journey. Meanwhile, the crowd tagged along behind him. He turned to them and said, "Sorry to have kept you waiting." . . .

Said a member of the reception committee to one of the reporters, "That's the first time I ever saw a sermon walking."[18]

The late Erma Bombeck, one of my favorite folks, had a real gift for finding joy in every situation. One of her first jobs was writing obituaries at a newspaper—surely a job that was almost as dull as straightening staples and sorting golf balls! But Erma found a way to laugh about her situation. She told her friends how thrilled her mother was when she read the obituaries Erma had written. "She was so impressed that I got all the victims to die in alphabetical order," Erma joked. And she once quipped that the epitaph she wanted on her own gravestone was:

Big deal! I'm used to dust.

Oh, to have Erma's joyful attitude—the same joyful mind-set of the little girl in another Henri Nouwen story. Nouwen was studiously interviewing an artist when the woman's little five-year-old daughter came bustling into the room. "I made a birthday cake with sand," she told him sweetly. "Now you have to come and pretend that you're eating it and that you like it. That will be fun!"

The little girl's mother smiled at Nouwen and said to him, "You'd better play with her before you talk to me. Maybe she has more to teach you than I have."[19]

Some of us need to learn how to be God's joyful crown-wearers—and our teachers don't have to be Nobel Prize winners to teach us this lesson! They may even be innocent children, who so often seem to possess a natural gift for laughter. Our responsibility is to make ourselves teachable!

A Crown-Wearer's Duties

If we were royal heirs to an earthly monarch, we might have grand, attention-getting duties such as leading military campaigns or reigning over lavish ceremonial affairs. Instead, we are heirs to a servant King, whom we honor by serving others in humility and in love. Our responsibilities may not be glorious deeds that win us loud acclaim—at least not on this side of heaven. Here, our tasks may be something much simpler—and even more important:

> To speak a healing word to a broken heart.
> To extend a hand to one who has fallen.
> To give a smile to those whose laughter has
>   been lost.
> To encourage the dreamer who has given up.
> To share the painful solitude of one who is alone.
> To ease the burden of one bent low beneath a
>   thankless task.
> To reassure the doubter and reinforce the
>   believer.
> To light the candle of God's Word in the midst
>   of another's darkest night.

There's an inspiring story about a man who was disheartened by all the sorrow he saw in the world around him. Everywhere he looked he saw the evidence of our broken world: abandoned children, abusive marriages, desperate men and women suffering unspeakable pain.

In frustration, the distraught man cried out, "God, why don't You *do* something?"

"I have," God replied quietly. "I created you."

Crowns with Chin Straps

Our heavenly crowns may be glorious ornaments we'll wear while singing praises to our King when we get to heaven, but here on earth, Christ's crown of servanthood should come with a chin strap, because we have a lot of work to do! A friend sent me an essay recently that describes the "doodles" that appear on another woman's prayer journal. One of the drawings is a crown, drawn there to remind her, as she prays for her children, that "what they are today is not what they will be tomorrow." The same is true for all of us. And it just may be that WE are the instruments He's using to love or encourage someone else. As this writer said, "God Himself is at work in [all of us] and He will complete what He has begun." Her thoughts echo the wisdom of the apostle John, who wrote:

> If anyone acknowledges that Jesus is the Son of God, God lives in him and he in God. . . . God is love. Whoever lives in love lives in God, and God in him. In this way, love is made complete among us so that we will have confidence on the day of judgment, because in this world we are like him.[20]

God the Father is our King. Like Him, we will someday wear a crown of glory. We'll find it waiting for us when we arrive at the foot of His throne. There will be no need for fittings, no delay for customizing. God knows our head size!

Cloud Busters

> For the LORD takes delight in his people;
> he crowns the humble with salvation.[21]

"Oh, how I wish the Lord would come during my lifetime!" Queen Victoria of England told one of her advisers.

When he asked why, "her countenance brightened, and with deep emotion she replied, 'Because I would love to lay my crown at His blessed feet in reverent adoration.'"[22]

The Earliest Smile of Day

Oh, look! the Savior blest,
Calm after solemn rest,
Stands in the garden 'neath His olive boughs.
The earliest smile of day
Doth on his vesture play,
And light the majesty of his still brows;
While angels hang with wings outspread,
Holding the new-worn crown above his
    saintly head.

Jean Ingelow

In mansions of glory and endless delight,
I'll ever adore Thee in heaven so bright;
I'll sing with the glittering crown on my brow;
If ever I loved Thee, my Jesus, 'tis now.

William R. Featherstone

I've no idea when Jesus is coming back. I'm on the Welcoming Committee, not the Planning Committee.[23]

Soon after *Geranium* was published, I was invited to speak at David Jeremiah's large church in San Diego, where the "ticket" to get in was to wear some kind of crazy hat. What fun it was to stand at the podium and look out over that sea of zaniness crowning the heads of fifteen hundred ladies! One woman's hat was even battery-powered, with lights that blinked and flashed. But the idea that stole the show was one woman's portrayal of laughter in life's cesspools. On her head she wore an upside-down bedpan, decorated with geraniums!

It takes many hours to fill a pail of water if you're doing it drop by drop. Even when the pail seems full, it can take many drops more. Eventually, of course, one drop more makes the pail overflow.

So it is with kindness. Most people appreciate even one deed of kindness, but some find it difficult to show their appreciation. Don't let this stop you. Eventually you'll do some little thing that will make their hearts overflow.[24]

Finish then Thy new creation,
Pure and spotless let us be;
Let us see Thy great salvation,
Perfectly restored in Thee;
Changed from Glory into glory,
Till in heaven we take our place,
Till we cast our crowns before Thee,
Lost in wonder, love, and praise!

Charles Wesley, "Love Divine"

Never give up! The iron crown of suffering precedes the golden crown of glory.

According to your latest figures, if you retired today, you could live very, very comfortably until about 2 p.m. tomorrow.

The wealth of the wise is their crown.[25]

I've got a mansion just over the hilltop,
In that bright land where we'll never grow old;
And someday yonder we will nevermore wander,
But walk on streets that are purest gold.[1]

Finally, Fabulously *Home!*

The phone rang one day when my arms were loaded with mail and packages I'd just brought home from the post office. Grabbing the receiver off the wall phone as I passed it in the hall, I heard a voice say, "Oh, Barb! I've just got to talk to you! I've been trying to get your phone number for days, and finally I found you!"

Juggling my load of paperwork from one arm to the other, I squeezed the phone between my shoulder and chin. "Wait a minute," I said. "I've gotta get to another phone where I can sit down. Can you hang on a minute?"

"Okay," she replied.

Leaving the phone dangling by its cord, I hurried to unload the mail onto my desk. Then, on my way to the living room, my eye fell on some letters I'd intended to put outside for the mailman (we get mail both at home and at the post office). It just took a second to slip outside and stick them in the—Oops! The mail had already been picked up, and more had been delivered. Scooping the new stuff out of the box, I

trotted back into the house and piled it on the table and suddenly remembered the finished cycle of clothes still waiting
in the washer. Moving quickly, I loaded them into the dryer
and then scooted into my Joy Room so I could ride my exer-
cise bike while we talked on the phone.

"I'm back!" I panted into the phone, exhausted by all my
running.

"How come it took you so long to go from one phone to the
other?" the woman asked rather indignantly. "I thought you
just lived in a mobile home!"

Folks have all sorts of images of mobile homes, I guess.
This woman apparently imagined that Bill and I lived in a
camper-sized trailer. It's not small—or at least it doesn't seem
small when I have to clean it! And it's set in a lovely park that
has a beautiful lake with sculptured landscaping and water
fountains, and a large swimming pool and Jacuzzi. So it's not
exactly what most people picture when they think of a "trailer
park." We sold our home and moved here twenty-one years
ago when the kids were gone so that we could have the comfort and convenience of a leisurely lifestyle. At that time we
had no inkling that Spatula Ministries would be born and that
we would be traveling constantly. But in God's economy, that
was part of His plan for us, and we love the freedom we have
here and all the pleasures that go with it.

We built a large Joy Room onto our home that makes a most
unique guestroom with lots of toys and signs and hanging
things designed to make us laugh.

A few years ago we welcomed into our Joy Room the heart-
broken mother of a son dying with AIDS. She had traveled
clear across the country to California for a special meeting of
our local Spatula support group. She rode with us in our ten-
year-old Volvo from the meeting back to our home that night
and then settled happily into the Joy Room, thanking us pro-
fusely for making her feel so welcome. The woman was a
most gracious guest, delighted with all the silly knickknacks
surrounding her. Occasionally as she got ready for bed we
could hear her out there, chuckling at something she'd just
spotted in the corner or hanging on the wall.

A few months later, when I had a speaking engagement near her home in Florida, the woman invited us to spend a couple of nights with her so she could "return the hospitality," as she said. She picked me up where I was speaking and drove me to her home in a new, luxurious car. As soon as we turned into her neighborhood, I was amazed by the huge size of the homes there. They were MANSIONS!

When she welcomed us into her lovely home, I was nearly breathless with the wonder of the many large rooms, the lavish furnishings, and the exquisitely detailed decor. Her home had a gorgeous spiral staircase like you might see in the movies, and her dining room looked like the one I'd seen at the Hearst Castle. There were even servants who waited on us with sweet southern hospitality and provided every comfort we might want.

The most spectacular thing about her mansion was the atrium, which was larger than my entire mobile home. It had a huge ficus tree that had been specially designed just for that entryway. It was more than forty feet tall and had been crafted from a cypress trunk with three enormous branches. More than twenty-five thousand silk leaves had been individually attached with hot glue, making the tree spread out to fill the atrium. It sort of reminded me of the huge Swiss Family Robinson tree at Disneyland where kids can climb up and play. Thinking of all those silk leaves being glued on one by one just sort of overwhelmed me. Her whole mansion overwhelmed me!

As I unpacked in the spacious guestroom, I thought of how humble and appreciative my friend had been to settle in so contentedly, sleeping in a meager single bed in our Joy Room. She had her own bathroom at our house, but it was a miniature-sized cubbyhole adjoining the Joy Room, certainly nothing luxurious like she had at home. Still, she had bubbled with laughter, considering it lots of fun to visit with us. *Boy! What a far cry she was from her own deluxe furnishings,* I thought, looking at her fabulous home and remembering how graciously she had settled into my mobile-home Joy Room with all its tacky toys and signs.

Since then, these contrasting images—my friend's stay in our humble Joy Room and my incredulous arrival at her fabulous mansion—have dissolved into heavenly visions in my mind. When I think of my friend leaving her mansion to come visit me in my modest mobile home, I imagine Jesus leaving the glorious neighborhoods of heaven to come to a humble Bethlehem barn. Remembering the wonder of my friend's beautiful mansion, I realize that, as beautiful as it was, the mansion waiting for us in heaven would make her luxurious home seem like a tar-paper shack.

"Barb, we'll know how to find you in heaven. Your mansion will have geraniums all around it!"

Heavenly Homes

As different as they are from each other as well as from the palaces awaiting us in glory, my friend's mansion and my mobile home *do* have at least one thing in common with those divine domiciles in heaven: They're *both* filled with love.

If you grew up in a loving family, you're probably familiar with that strong, nurturing sense of welcome that wraps around you the instant you step inside the door. It's an atmosphere, a comforting feeling, that engulfs you like a soft cloud of warm, soothing mist. It's the sound of footsteps rushing toward you, the tinkle of laughter bubbling up from someone who's glad to see you. It's the light in a window and the sparkle in a loved one's eyes. In short, it's *home*.

That's surely the feeling, multiplied ten thousand times, that we'll have as we fly through the clouds and find ourselves in heaven. What joy we'll experience! What a welcome we'll receive! What love we'll know! All these glorious feelings will flood over us, and we'll be spellbound with the wonder of it all. Best of all, we'll finally hear the Master say those two precious words we've longed for through all of earth's trials: *"Welcome HOME!"*

Hallelujah Square

Yes, there's a welcome waiting for us in heaven that will exceed any reception we've ever known as human beings. It's beyond our imagination. Still, it's fun to think about, isn't it? One of the most heartwarming ideas about how heaven's entryway will look adorns the extraordinary, floor-to-ceiling "Hallelujah Square" murals in the beautiful Precious Moments Chapel near Carthage, Missouri.

The murals depict a "child's view of heaven" in the chapel built by Sam Butcher, the artist and creator of the adorable Precious Moments figures that have charmed millions of collectors around the world. Sam has graciously given me several of these delightful characters to share as illustrations in this book.

The idea of building the chapel occurred to Sam when he visited the magnificent Sistine Chapel in Rome several years ago. But standing in the famous church, Sam noticed that the tourists around him didn't seem emotionally connected to

Michelangelo's beautiful masterpiece that stretches across the ceiling. They simply admired the famous scene and then moved on, their faces expressionless. Sam was inspired in that great place to create a chapel himself to express his own gratitude to God. But he wanted it to be a place where visitors' hearts would be touched by the experience.

Soon after his visit to Rome, Sam was on the West Coast on business. He had a return airline ticket, but at the last minute he decided to rent a car and drive cross-country, sensing God directing him in this change of plans. He prayed as he drove, and by the end of the second or third day he was in the middle of America on his way back to Grand Rapids, Michigan. It was late at night, and as he traveled northeast on I-44 through the edge of the Ozarks, his headlights shone on an exit sign for highway HH.

Somehow that sign—highway HH—seemed significant to Sam, but he didn't understand why. Almost before he knew what was happening, he found himself turning the car around and heading back to the nearest motel to spend the night. Despite the late hour, he called a friend and said, "I think I've found a place for the chapel."

"That's great!" the friend replied. "Where are you?"

"Well," admitted Sam, "I don't really know."

The next morning he went to a real estate office. Several agents happened to be in the office that morning, all dressed in nice business suits. Sam was wearing faded blue jeans and a casual shirt. He explained to them that he was looking for a place to build a beautiful chapel. The agents, of course, wanted to know how he would pay for such a project. But they didn't wait for a reply. Instead, they basically ignored Sam, returning to their own conversation.

Sam was embarrassed. He knew he should leave, but somehow he just couldn't seem to make his feet move. Standing there in confusion, he caught the eye of the receptionist and could see that she was embarrassed for him. With a smile, he finally turned toward the door. But before he reached it he felt a hand on his shoulder. It was an older agent who'd overheard

Sam's description. "I think I know a place that's just what you're describing," he said. "C'mon. Let's go check it out."

Grateful to be rescued from the awkward predicament, Sam hopped into the car with the agent, and soon they were winding their way through the hills. As they rode, they got acquainted. And they learned that they shared the same strong Christian convictions. Soon the agent, Mel Brown, slowed the car to make a turn, and as he did, Sam looked hard at the road sign before them. They were turning onto highway HH.

"Where are we going?" Sam asked.

"This is where the property is that I want to show you," Mel replied.

"And what's this road HH? What does that mean?"

"Well, here in Missouri, we label the county roads with letters. This is a county road, and its name is HH. It doesn't really mean anything official. But I've always thought of it as 'heaven's highway.'"

All Sam could do was smile.

Soon they turned onto a winding dirt road and parked on a sloping hillside. They had walked only a short way when Sam stopped and scanned the landscape before him. At that moment he envisioned a chapel—the chapel that is now a reality and has drawn more than seven million visitors in its few years of existence.

Sam bought seventeen and a half acres that very day.

He wrote a check for the full amount.

Today the beautiful chapel, set amidst the rolling Ozark hills, welcomes visitors through its intricately carved doors. Inside, fifty-two biblical murals and thirty exquisite stained-glass windows inspire young and old alike. But the most remarkable thing about the sanctuary is that few people venture inside without having their hearts touched in some way. (Boxes of tissues are discreetly placed throughout the building for those who find tears mysteriously rolling down their cheeks. Judging by the reaction of the people who were there when I visited, the chapel staff must go through lots of tissues!)

The artwork lining the walls and stretching across the beautiful ceiling depicts the sweet little Precious Moments characters, and there's a story behind every picture. It is all so touching. But the most amazing feature of the chapel is that set of three magnificent murals at the front of the chapel—Hallelujah Square. It's an inspiring scene that quickly brought to my mind the chorus of a beautiful song:

> I'll see all my friends in Hallelujah Square.
> What a wonderful time we'll all have up there:
> We'll sing and praise Jesus, His glory to share,
> And we'll all live forever in Hallelujah Square.[2]

Many of the little Precious Moments figurines that have charmed so many folks around the world are based on actual people. That's also true of many of the Precious Moments angels depicted in Hallelujah Square; their namesakes are identified in photographs displayed in another room in the chapel. It's a touching symbol of how God uses the broken pieces of our lives, in this case it's often broken hearts, to create a beautiful comfort blanket of love.

For example, a little, dark-haired soldier-angel standing solemnly before the American flag was inspired by a decorated World War II veteran who was tormented for decades after the war by memories of the violence he believed he'd been forced to commit during the conflict. He wanted to believe in Jesus, but he felt unworthy. No one had ever told Sergeant Thomas about the wonderful gift of God's all-encompassing grace.

The sergeant's daughter had been led to the Lord many years earlier by Sam Butcher. So when, on his death bed, her father asked her, "Sissy, do you think Jesus loves me? Could He love even me?" she said she was "ready to tell him of God's love and of Jesus' sacrifice so that we can all be forgiven."

Now, when tour guides point out the features of the poignant mural, they sometimes tell the story of the little soldier standing with his comrades in Hallelujah Square. His presence there, inside heaven's gates, affirms the daughter's answer to her father's question: "Yes, Daddy, Jesus loves you. The Bible tells me so!"[3]

The mural shows the little angels doing things they loved to do—or weren't physically able to do because of disabilities—when they lived on earth. There is a comforting atmosphere of joy in Sam Butcher's portrayal of heaven as seen through the eyes of a child. When one of my friends saw the murals, she said the scene gave her a whole new attitude toward life in the hereafter. Before, she said, she had thought of heaven as a reverently majestic, praise-filled place. After seeing the little Precious Moments angels frolicking around Hallelujah Square, she also thought of it as a haven where we will share laughter—and *fun.*

Light and Love

Another mural in the Precious Moments Chapel depicts Sam Butcher's son, who was killed a few years ago in a car crash, arriving at those gates. The greeters there are holding another set of signs that say, "Welcome home, Philip." What a joy that will be to arrive in such a beautiful glorious place—and be greeted by name. Better yet, we'll instantly feel *at home*, immediately recognizing that enveloping *familiar* warmth of comfort surrounding us like a comfort blanket.

One of the familiar images I associate with memories of my childhood home is a porch light reflecting on snow. Growing up in Michigan, I'm on a first-name basis with snow and ice! One of my most cherished images is of walking home at night, strolling along the snowy sidewalks as we returned from church or some other outing. Nearing our neighborhood, I could spot my home from quite a ways off. Light would be streaming out the windows, making the snow glisten on our front lawn like transient diamonds scattered on the ground.

You probably have similar memories—of returning from someplace at night and seeing your home from a long way off or of turning a corner and suddenly seeing it there before you. To weary travelers—and even to those who've been away just a short while—the light of home can cut through the darkest night in a way that's different from all other sources of illumination. It flashes out a greeting of warmth, welcoming us back from the cold, winter night. Imagine that feeling magnified ten thousand times, and that's the light that will welcome us as we approach the gates of heaven.

Perhaps my memory of light beaming through the windows of our childhood home is why I appreciate so much the glowing houses and cottages in Thomas Kinkade's marvelous paintings. His pictures remind me of *home*. And right now I know I'm nearer my *heavenly* home than my childhood home.

In other words, to me,

Home is spelled H-E-A-V-E-N!

And we know that the light pouring out of heaven, extending a warm welcome to all those who know and love the Lord, is none other than God Himself. He is the *real* reason why heaven will be so wonderful. As fabulous as they'll be, our mansions will really be just dwelling places. The angelic choir, as much as it will resonate throughout the universe, will just be background music. The streets of gold, the pearly gates, and all those other beautiful images we may hold of paradise will just be window dressing.

A Home Made with Love

There will be beautiful things in heaven, but even if those things weren't going to be there, even if the only "thing" there was God, that would be enough. Because He loves us as no one else could ever love us. And when we're wrapped in that love, nothing else matters.

A clipping someone sent me provides a human illustration of the love Jesus is building into our heavenly mansions. It describes how a church and youth group in Iowa bought three hundred two-by-fours for a local Habitat for Humanity project. Before the lumber was used in framing the house, the thoughtful Christians "inscribed the lumber with messages of joy to the future homeowners."[4]

Knowing that the very framework of your home was inscribed with Scripture verses and messages of love and joy, how could you be anything but joyful each time you entered? That's surely how our mansions in heaven will feel to us as we step through the front doors, knowing that place is infused with love.

But even though we know in our hearts that, as someone said,

Heaven's delights will far outweigh
any difficulties we encounter here on earth,

we can't help but be distracted from that knowledge sometimes. It seems absurd that earthly worries could keep us from relishing the knowledge of what's in store for us in heaven—but they do. Sometimes it's the silliest notions that pull our focus off of what's important and set us on a truly trivial pursuit.

A story told by aviator Charles Lindbergh's daughter, Reeve Lindbergh, illustrates how easy it is to be consumed with insignificant things while ignoring something wonderful that's easily within our reach.

In 1997 Reeve was invited to give the annual Lindbergh Address at the Smithsonian Institution's Air and Space Museum to commemorate the seventieth anniversary of her father's historic solo flight across the Atlantic. On the day of the speech, museum officials invited her to come early, before the facility opened, so that she could have a closeup look at *The Spirit of St. Louis*, the little plane, suspended from the museum ceiling, that her father had piloted from New York to Paris in 1927.

That morning in the museum, Reeve and her young son, Ben, eagerly climbed into the bucket of a cherry-picker, a long-armed crane that carried them upward until the plane was at eye level and within their reach. Seeing the machine that her father had so bravely flown across the sea was an unforgettable experience for Reeve. She had never touched the plane before, and that morning, twenty feet above the floor of the museum, she tenderly reached out to run her fingers along the door handle, which she knew her father must have grasped many times with his own hand.

Tears welled up in her eyes at the thought of what she was doing. "Oh, Ben," she whispered, her voice trembling, "isn't this amazing?"

"Yeaaaaaah," Ben replied, equally impressed. "I've never been in a cherry-picker before!"[5]

Carrying Empty Freight

How often do we get distracted by some insignificant problem or event down here on earth and let our focus drift away from heaven and the One who waits for us there? As someone said, "We need to keep the Main Thing the main thing!" And the "Main Thing" is Jesus!

Yet, like Charles Lindbergh's grandson, we can be derailed by silly distractions that pull our focus away from what's really important. Or we can get hung up on activities and even worship schedules that, in the beginning, bring us closer to God. But when they're repeated exactly the same way over and over again, they can become monotonous. So our daily devotions become flat and uninspired, or we leave a church service and find that we can't even remember the lesson that was taught. But we just keep doing the same thing the same way because it's become a routine—a regimen we follow without thinking, a treadmill to nowhere rather than an elevator transporting our thoughts heavenward. That's when we have to shake ourselves awake and jump-start our worship, prayer time, or devotions.

At one of the Women of Faith conferences, the speakers had to climb three flights of steep stairs to go "the back way" from the floor of the arena up to the concourse where our books were being sold. Climbing all those stairs was no fun, so I looked around for an elevator. But the only elevator in the whole building was marked with a big, stern-looking sign that said, "This Elevator for Freight Only."

I looked at that sign, then I looked over my shoulder—and pushed the button! The oversized doors of the elevator yawned open vertically, like a huge whale swallowing up its prey. And I, feeling a little like Jonah, stepped inside.

The elevator carried me up and down between the arena floor and the concourse several times that day. Then, late in the afternoon, the elevator doors opened, and a workman and several boxes were waiting inside. As I'd been doing all day, I stepped inside, but the workman told me firmly, "Sorry, ma'am. This elevator is only for freight."

He had his hand on the control panel as if to clearly indicate which one of us was in charge.

"Oh, it's all right," I assured him with my brightest smile. "I've been riding it all day. You see, I'm one of the speakers, and I only have a few minutes to get upstairs to the book table before I have to be back on stage."

"Sorry, ma'am," he said again, pointing to the fine print under the "Freight Only" sign that explained it was the fire marshal's idea, not his. "You've gotta have freight to ride on this elevator. That's what the regulations say."

As in most situations where I'm not getting my way, my next step was whining. "Oh, please!" I moaned. "I've been using this elevator all day. It hasn't bothered anyone else."

"I'm really sorry, ma'am. It's the rule," he replied adamantly.

Obediently, I stepped out of the elevator. Then I spied something through the doorway of the nearby ladies room. "Wait a minute!" I yelled over my shoulder. Then, hurrying into the restroom, I grabbed a huge, *empty* cardboard box that once had held bathroom tissue. Folding the flaps down and holding them in place with my chin, I hurried back out to the elevator. Barely able to see over the top as I clutched the empty box in my arms, I stepped awkwardly into the whale's mouth and turned confidently to face the front, waiting for the jaws to snap shut. "Okay," I said merrily. "I got some freight! Now I'm qualified to ride!"

Apparently satisfied that I was now in compliance with the rules, the man pushed a button on the control panel, the elevator gate and jaws closed, and up we went!

As the metal beast rumbled upward through the elevator shaft to the concourse, the thought suddenly occurred to me that we're fortunate God doesn't require us to bring along any "freight" when we head toward heaven. As the beloved old song says, "Nothing in my hand I bring, simply to your cross I cling."[6]

Last year I noticed a touching photograph in a magazine that poignantly illustrated that fact. The picture accompanied a story about the powerful floods that had devastated parts of North Dakota and Minnesota in 1997. The focal point of the picture was a large sign leaning up against a pile of rubble—lumber, insulation, soaked carpet, and ruined appliances that had been pulled from one of the flood-stricken homes. In bold, black letters the sign said, "Store your treasures in HEAVEN!"[7]

*This sign outside an empty, flood-stricken house
offered a lesson in faith.*

That lesson reminds me of the quip that says:

> The average person probably hasn't stored up
> enough treasure in heaven to even make a down
> payment for a harp!

When I think of all the *things* we consider important here
on earth and the luxury we'll enjoy in heaven not having to
worry about all our *stuff* anymore, I feel like kicking up my

heels and dancing a jig! Won't it be nice not to have to tend to all those dust-catchers and anxiety-inducers anymore? We won't have to worry about getting a dent in the minivan, a leak in the roof, or a bug in the computer. We won't have to fret about some cherished antique getting scratched or some inherited jewelry getting lost. No more frustration about snagged pantyhose or stained shirts. No more lost eyeglasses, misplaced hearing aids, or left-behind checkbooks. Why, just thinking about living in a place where I'll *never* have to search for my car keys again makes me downright giddy! What freedom we'll enjoy when released from bondage to all the *things* that have held us captive here on earth!

And even when we talk of storing our "treasures" in heaven rather than on earth, we know we're talking about two very different kinds of treasures. The thing we'll cherish most in heaven won't be a *thing* at all. It will be living in the presence of our loving Father and Creator. In fact, our palaces in heaven probably won't need any closets. After all, we're not going to bring any earthly treasures along with us. And we won't be bringing along any emotional baggage, either, when we're heading off for paradise, because Jesus says we're to lay down our burdens and let *Him* carry the freight!

> Come unto me, all ye that labour and are heavy laden, and I will give you rest.[8]

Just imagine living where love fills our lives so completely there won't be any empty spaces left in us to fill. Therefore we won't *want* anything. We'll be perfectly content—supremely satisfied. And since that will surely be the case, it seems quite likely that our heavenly palaces won't need to be very big because we won't have any *stuff* to store. They may be like the tiny little church shown in a newspaper photograph someone sent me. The caption says the minuscule Christ's Chapel Church, located in South Newport, Georgia, has welcomed passers-by for fifty years. Complete with peaked roof, beautiful stained-glass windows, and a stand-alone bell "tower," the little chapel in the photograph looks almost like a child's playhouse. The rows on either side of the center aisle are only two chairs wide, so it seems doubtful that even a dozen people could squeeze inside. But people do stop there, probably because the church's motto touches their hearts. The tiny chapel has proclaimed itself to be a place "where folks rub elbows with God."[9]

That photograph of the little church was the idea that made me rethink my vision of the palace awaiting me in heaven. Maybe it will be a *petite palace*—a wonderfully comfortable and inviting place—without being large and *palatial*. Maybe it'll be a small, warm, cozy place where I can rub elbows with God.

Whatever the Lord has prepared for me, I know it will be wonderful. As someone said, "I don't need to know the floor plan and decor. It is enough that [Jesus] has promised that He will come and take me to Himself. . . . There will be room for me, and it will be a bountiful homecoming."[10]

In heaven we won't be encumbered by all the material goods that clutter our lives here on earth. Whatever their size, our heavenly homes will be places of love set in neighborhoods where the peace is never interrupted by police or ambulance sirens, storm warnings, or blaring security alarms. How wonderful it is to picture the happy life we'll know for all eternity. How comforting it is to know we'll share it with our friends and loved ones who are waiting for us there.

One of my friends who shares my eager anticipation for heaven said she hopes we can be neighbors there. "Barb, I hope our mansions have kitchen windows that face each other," she said gleefully.

For years, I've shared a letter written by Dr. Harry Rimmer after he was on a radio show hosted by Dr. Charles Fuller. As far as I can tell, the story of the letter was first recorded by Al Smith of Greenville, South Carolina. Apparently, as Dr. Fuller was closing his radio program on the day Dr. Rimmer participated, he mentioned that the following week's show would focus on heaven. Later, Dr. Rimmer wrote Dr. Fuller this letter:

My Dear Charlie,

Next Sunday you are to talk about heaven. I am interested in that land, because I have held a clear title to a bit of property there for over fifty years. I did not buy it. It was given to me without money and without price. But the donor purchased it for me at tremendous cost.

I am not holding it for speculation, for the deed is not transferable. It is not a vacant lot, for I have been sending materials there for over fifty years out of which the greatest Architect and Builder of the universe has been building a home for me that will suit me perfectly and will never need to be repaired.

Termites cannot undermine its foundations, for it rests upon the "Rock of Ages."

Fire cannot destroy it.

Floods cannot wash it away.

No locks or bolts will ever be placed upon its doors, for no devious person can ever enter that land where my dwelling now stands, almost completed.

It is ready for me to enter in and rest in peace eternally without fear of being ejected.

There is a valley of deep shadow between the place where I live in California and that to which I shall journey in a short time. I cannot reach my home in that city of gold without passing through this dark valley of shadows. But I am not afraid, because the best Friend I ever had went through the same valley long ago and drove away its gloom. He has stuck with me through thick and thin since we first became acquainted fifty-five years ago, and I hold His promise in printed form never to forsake me nor to leave me alone. He will be with me as I walk through the valley of the shadows, and I shall not lose my way when He is with me.

I hope to hear your sermon on Sunday next from my home here, but I have no assurance that I shall.

My ticket to heaven has no date stamped upon it,
no return coupon, and no permit for baggage. I am
all ready to go, and I may not be here when you are
talking next Sunday, but if not, I shall meet you
there someday.

According to the story, this letter arrived at Dr. Fuller's
home on Wednesday. But "by that time, Dr. Rimmer was
already in that land which is fairer than day, the land he had
seen by faith for over fifty years."[11]

Like Dr. Rimmer, I've spent many years looking, by faith,
at the heavenly real estate that's waiting for me. How wonderful to know that I've got a "mansion just over the hilltop,
in that bright land where we'll never grow old." It won't be
long, now, before the housewarming committee welcomes me
to a moving-in party. And what a celebration that will be! This
beautiful poem says it so well:

When I Come Home to Heaven

When I come home to Heaven
How joyful it will be!
For on that day at last
My risen Lord I'll see.

No greater happiness than
To see Him face to face,
To see the love in His eyes
And feel His warm embrace.

I've done nothing to deserve
That perfect home above.
It was given freely through
The grace of Jesus' love.

Then why should earthly cares
Weigh down upon me so?

They'll be a distant memory
When home at last I go.

Beth Stuckwisch,
© 1984 Dicksons.
Used by permission.

Cloud Busters

The way to heaven:
Turn right at Calvary and keep going straight!

This bumper sticker was punctuated with a bold cross:
No matter which direction I'm heading,
I'm homeward bound!

A woman was dying in the poorhouse. The doctor bent over her and heard her whisper, "Praise the Lord."

"Why, auntie," he said, "how can you praise God when you are dying in a poorhouse?"

"Oh, doctor," she replied, "it's wonderful to go from the poorhouse to a mansion in the skies!"[12]

A reporter watched a fire consume a house. He noticed a little boy with his mom and dad. The reporter, fishing for a human interest angle, said to the boy, "Son, it looks as if you don't have a home anymore."

The boy answered brightly, "We have a home. We just don't have a house to put it in."[13]

Home, where house ten thousand angels.
Home, where the most silent of prayers were heard.
Home, where my beloved Savior now awaits.
Finally, finally, home.

Roger Shouse

I am home in heaven, dear ones;
All's so happy, all's so bright!
There's perfect joy and beauty
In this everlasting light.

All the pain and grief are over,
Every restless tossing passed;
I am now at peace forever,
Safely home in heaven at last.

Did you wonder how I so calmly
Trod the Valley of the Shade?
Oh! But Jesus' love illumined
Every dark and fearful glade.

And He came Himself to meet me
In that way so hard to tread;
And with Jesus' arm to lean on,
Could I have one doubt or dread?

Then you must not grieve so sorely;
For I love you dearly still;
Try to look beyond earth's shadows,
Pray to trust our Father's will.

There is work still waiting for you,
So you must not idle stand;
Do your work while life remaineth—
You shall rest in Jesus' land.

When that work is all completed,
He will gently call you home.
Oh, the rapture of the meeting!
Oh, the joy to see you come!

Source Unknown

Thank heavens we won't have to decipher any "creative" real estate jargon (like the samples below) when we get to heaven!

Charming: Tiny. Snow White might fit, but five of the dwarfs would have to find their own place.

Unique City Home: Used to be a warehouse.

Daring Design: Still a warehouse.

Completely Updated: Avocado dishwasher and harvest gold carpeting.

One-of-a-Kind: Ugly as sin.

Must See to Believe: An absolutely accurate understatement.[14]

At dusk a little girl entered a cemetery. An old man who sat at the gate said to her, "Aren't you afraid to go through the cemetery in the dark?"

"Oh no," she replied. "My home is just on the other side."

Many folks buy cemetery lots in advance but do nothing about preparing a home in heaven.

Think . . .
of stepping on the shore
and finding it heaven;
of taking hold of a hand
and finding it God's hand;
of breathing a new air
and finding it celestial air;
of feeling invigorated
and finding it immortality;
of passing from storm and tempest
to an unknown calm;
of waking and finding you're Home!

Source Unknown

Jesus was content to be born in a stable so that we may have a mansion when we die.

Death is the golden key
that opens the palace of eternity.

Milton

Let not your heart be troubled: ye believe in God, believe also in me. In my Father's house are many mansions: if it were not so, I would have told you. I go to prepare a place for you. And if I go and prepare a place for you, I will come again, and receive you unto myself; that where I am, there ye may be also.[15]

Holy, holy, is what the angels sing,
And I expect to help them
Make the courts of heaven ring;
But when I sing redemption's story
They will fold their wings,
For angels never felt the joys
That our salvation brings.[1]

Angels Watchin' Over Me

During the week of his eightieth birthday, Billy Graham appeared on *Larry King Live* to discuss "life after fifty." Midway through the interview, Larry King asked, "Billy, what happens when you die?"

Billy responded confidently, "I believe that an angel will take me by the hand at that moment and take me into the presence of Christ." And then he added, "I'm looking forward to it with tremendous anticipation."[2]

In His parable about the rich man and the beggar named Lazarus who lived beside the rich man's gate, Jesus said Lazarus "died and the angels carried him to Abraham's side" in heaven.[3] Jesus also said when the Son of Man comes "on the clouds of the sky, with power and great glory," He will "send his angels with a loud trumpet call, and they will gather his elect from the four winds, from one end of the heavens to the other."[4]

One way or the other, it sounds like angels are assigned to escort us from earth to eternity. Stories abound of persons who, as they sigh out their last earthly breath, die with the happiest expressions on their faces. Isn't it amazing to think perhaps they're greeting that heavenly messenger who's been sent to fetch them home to heaven? As C. S. Lewis's beloved wife, Joy, drew her last breath, "she smiled," he said, "but not at me."[5] The last words of another woman thrill me every time I read them. She exclaimed, as she stepped from this world to the next, "How bright the room! How full of angels!"[6]

THE FAMILY CIRCUS   **By Bil Keane**

©1999 BKI

"If somebody dies in the hospital, angels move them to the eternity ward."

© Bil Keane

Just imagine seeing those celestial beings coming toward us, calling us by name, escorting us through the clouds to the throne of God! And when we get there, we'll find heaven *teeming* with angels. The Bible says there will be "thousands upon thousands, and ten thousand times ten thousand" of angels there.[7]

One Bible scholar speculates that "there may be as many angels as there are stars in the heavens, for angels are associated with the stars [in several Bible passages]. If this be so, there would exist untold *trillions* of these heavenly beings." And all of them, he believes, "possess separate and individual personalities, probably no two alike."[8]

And all those angels aren't there just to look pretty. They work! Their first "job" in heaven, just as ours will be, is to praise God. But, just as we'll inevitably do ourselves, they have other work too. One of their jobs, scholars say, is to "act as intermediaries between God and humans."[9] This is a role angels have performed since the beginning of time, when God "placed on the east side of the Garden of Eden cherubim and a flaming sword flashing back and forth to guard the way to the tree of life."[10]

What intriguing assignments angels have had since then! Working under God's orders, an angel brought messages to the slave Hagar and her master, Abraham; warned Lot to flee from Gomorrah; beckoned Moses to the burning bush; and protected and guided the children of Israel as they fled from Egypt and then wandered in the wilderness. God sent an angel to block the road in front of Balaam and his donkey as they trod a reckless path, and He sent an angel to instruct Samson's mother-to-be in prenatal care.

The most exciting part of angelic assignments must be those missions when angels are called upon to perform daring and exciting rescues. Can't you just picture God's army of angels up in heaven, waiting eagerly for a new mission, wondering what exciting, life-changing event they'll be part of? Maybe they're hoping they can walk, unscathed, into a fiery furnace like the angel who rescued Shadrach, Meshach, and Abednego. Or perhaps they're hoping to bed down with the lions like the angel who spent the night with Daniel in the lions' den.

It would scare the wits out of anyone who hadn't been trained by God Himself to hear, "One of you must go into that terrible prison, unshackle Peter, and lead him out," or, best of all, "You're going to have to walk into the darkest, most terrible tomb of death that's ever existed . . . and roll that stone away from the door." Can't you just see the angels rejoicing over such assignments?

On the other hand, think what a joyful assignment it must have been for the angel who led Dr. V. Raymond Edman home to heaven in 1967. Sharon Barnes, my friend and co-worker on the Women of Faith tour, told me how Dr. Edman, chancellor of Wheaton College, was admired and loved by the students. That's why they were overjoyed when he returned, after recuperating several weeks from a heart attack, to speak during the college's chapel service in September. Dr. Edman told the students that day, "Chapel is a time of worship, a time of meeting the King." And then, a few seconds later, Dr. Edman paused and slumped forward over the podium as Sharon and the other college students watched in stunned silence. Then he dropped to the floor—and fell into the arms of that waiting angel to be gently ushered into the presence of God.

What Will *Our* Assignments Be?

Thinking about the work of the angels over the centuries makes us wonder what *our* jobs will be in heaven. Of course there's nothing in the Bible that says we become angels in heaven. And there's no way to know whether we'll even have assignments while we're devoting ourselves to the full-time praise of God. But since heaven is going to be a fulfilling and wonderful place, it makes sense to assume we'll be given something fulfilling and productive to do.

In her book *Heaven . . . Your Real Home,* Joni Eareckson Tada says confidently, "We will have jobs to do. . . . We will serve God through worship and work—exciting work of which we never grow tired."

Joni, who has been confined to a wheelchair for many years, adds, "For me, this will be heaven. I love serving God." She cites Jesus' heaven parable in Luke 19:17, which concludes with the master telling his servant, "'Well done, my good servant! . . . Because you have been trustworthy in a very small matter, take charge of ten cities.'"

From that, Joni reminds us, we believe that "those who are faithful in a few minor things will be put in charge over multitudinous things. . . . The more faithful you are in this life, the more responsibility you will be given in the life to come."[11] Joni also notes that we're promised "new heavens and a new earth" in Isaiah 65:17.

"Did you get that?" she asks. "Heaven has our planet in it. A new earth with earthy things in it. . . . warm and wonderful things that make earth . . . *earth.*"

And if that's the case, Joni has plans to do some things in her spare time that she's been unable to do since she was paralyzed in the accident. She says she has made dates with friends and relatives to climb the mountains behind the Rose Bowl, ski the Sierras, play doubles tennis, and dance. She's also looking forward to "picnicking on the Hungarian plains" with a circle of Rumanian orphan friends and racing a friend on horseback. Oh, and she's planning to do some knitting too.[12]

All she really needs to know, says Joni, is that "heaven will feel like home. I will be a co-heir with Christ. . . . I will help rule in the new heavens and the new earth . . . and I will be busier and happier in service than I ever dreamed possible. And you will be too."[13]

While We're Waiting . . .

Meanwhile, our job here on earth is to love and praise God— and our neighbors. In striving to do that, we can certainly draw inspiration (and ideas!) by following the example Jesus left us and also by studying the work of His angels.

Of course, the only real record of angelic visits is in the Bible. But Scripture seems to predict that angels continue to work in our lives today by reminding us, "Keep on loving each other as brothers. Do not forget to entertain strangers, for by so doing some people have entertained angels without knowing it."[14] It also asks us, as though assuming it's a fact we accept without questioning, "Are not all angels ministering spirits sent to serve those who will inherit salvation?"[15]

With these words echoing in our minds, many of us are constantly on the lookout for suspected angel contacts in our lives today. One woman told me that every time she sees a feather lying on the ground she's reminded that there are angels among us. Sure, she's knows it's just a bird's feather. But she uses each feather as a reminder, like a string tied around her finger, that the Bible assures us God has sent His angels to earth as our helpers and friends—usually invisible but, perhaps, sometimes appearing in flesh and blood. Billy Graham has said, "Angels speak. They appear and reappear. They are emotional creatures. While angels may become visible by choice, our eyes are not constructed to see them ordinarily any more than we can see the dimensions of a nuclear field, the structure of atoms or electricity."[16]

FAMILY CIRCUS

"That angel's name is Harold."

© Bil Keane

One of the most reassuring verses to me is:

> For He shall give His angels charge over you,
> To keep you in all your ways.

One of my friends calls this her biblical 911 number because of its source: Psalm 91:11.

Angels Among Us

Angels are one of my favorite things to think about. In fact, I've been collecting angels for quite a while now. My favorites are the ones that are blowing trumpets. That's where the idea for *Toot 'n' Scoot* originated. Now my Joy Room—actually, my whole home—is full of angels, including wall hangings, rugs, scarves, bookends, Christmas stockings, wall plaques, and eight or nine figurines that sit on the television! Everywhere I look I'm reminded that he's gonna toot and I'm gonna scoot. And that fact keeps me going when my energy is sagging along with my pantyhose and I'm ready to throw in the spatula! Along with collecting trumpet-blowing angels, I love reading or hearing about the ways angels are believed to have intervened in people's lives.

Because the Bible assures us that angels do, in fact, exist and that they minister to us, Christians often look for ways they can do angels' work too. In the rest of this chapter, I'd like to share some stories about people who believe they've been helped by angels—and people who were perceived as earthly angels sent by God to comfort others.

One of my favorite stories comes from a newsletter published by my friend Ney Bailey, a missionary with Campus Crusade for Christ, who has graciously agreed to share the story here. She calls it "one of the most motivating true-life stories in the area of prayer that I have ever heard," and I agree. She noted that the details of the story were confirmed several years ago by the missions chairman of the Boston church that supported the missionary involved in the dramatic account.

The missionary, Dr. Bob Foster, worked in Angola, a country where conflict between guerrilla forces opposing the Marxist regime made parts of the country especially dangerous. The medical clinic run by Dr. Foster was in one of these areas. Here is his story:

> One day Dr. Foster sent a co-worker on an errand to a city some miles away with the warning that he should be back by nightfall. The stretch of road between the clinic and the city went right through the jungle area where most of the guerrilla fighting took place, and it was very dangerous to travel through there at night.
>
> The co-worker went on his way, finished his errands in plenty of time, and began his return. Much to his dismay, however, his van developed engine trouble and broke down in the middle of the contested jungle area. With no other cars on the road, he had no choice but to lock the doors, pray, and attempt to get a little rest.
>
> Amazingly, he slept through to morning without a problem. He caught a ride into town for some spare parts, fixed the van, and completed the trip back to the clinic. He was greeted by a relieved Dr. Foster and other co-workers. "We are so thankful to see you!" Dr. Foster told him. "We heard sounds of heavy fighting from the area you were in." Dr. Foster's assistant said he had heard and seen nothing.
>
> Soon after that, a guerrilla officer came to the clinic to be treated. Curious, Dr. Foster asked him if he had seen a van stalled along the highway the previous night. "Yes, of course," replied the officer.
>
> "But why didn't you move in to take possession of it?" queried the doctor.
>
> "We started to," said the officer, "until we got closer. Then we saw that it was heavily guarded.

There were *twenty-seven* well-armed government soldiers surrounding it."

Needless to say, Dr. Foster and his co-worker were amazed.

The incident remained a mystery until Dr. Foster's assistant returned to the States on furlough. Here, person after person on his prayer team came up to him. . . . in fact, *twenty-seven people* in all [told him] the Lord had given them a special burden to pray for him on such-and-such a day previously. It was *the very day* he had been stranded in the jungle.

The story reminds us of that wonderful verse that says:

> The angel of the Lord encamps around those who fear Him, and rescues them.[17]

Ordinary, anonymous people who appear in our lives, do something wonderful, and then seem to vanish without a trace are assumed by many believers to be angels. Many such encounters are described in the Habitat for Humanity book, *The Excitement Is Building.* One of my favorite stories tells of an all-volunteer crew that was building a house in Fort Myers, Florida.

The volunteers arrived at the lot early one Saturday morning to assemble the prefabricated walls, door frames, and trusses. But when the walls were up and it was time to set the trusses—the big Vs that give the roof its peaked shape—"they simply would not fit," the authors wrote. The workers tried again and again to find ways to recalculate or relocate the trusses so they would fit, but it soon became apparent that the problem was impossible to remedy.

"About that time, a rather nondescript passerby stopped and looked over the situation. After a minute or two of thoughtful observation, he asked if he could survey the scene in more detail. Because everyone was so frustrated by this time, the man was hardly noticed as he scurried nimbly up the framework to examine the layout. He soon came down and gave all the dejected volunteers a jolt. He explained a detailed but basic solution to the seemingly unsolvable problem. The volunteers quickly set about doing just as he suggested, and his plan worked to perfection.

"And then they noticed that their 'Divine Engineer' had vanished."[18]

Being Angelic

The idea that angels are real, that they intercede in our world to minister to God's children (that's us!), should inspire us to do a little angel-work ourselves whenever the opportunity arises. The deeds we do don't always involve amazing mathematical calculations, like the work of the Habitat workers' "Divine Engineer." They can be as simple as a gentle word of encouragement or as quiet as a smile.

One thing I've learned is that God sometimes uses the smallest gestures of kindness to touch a life of torment, ease a broken heart, or light a spark of hope. My helpers and I see this happen at every Women of Faith conference when we give away the flat, shiny marbles I call "splashes of joy."

To be honest, these little gifts have gotten to be quite a job for us. They're shipped to each conference site by the manufacturer from Wichita, Kansas, and the boxes are *really* heavy. At the work space where my books will be sold, we risk wrenching our backs every time we lug one of the boxes up on the table—and there are usually several boxes of them.

Then, if we're lucky, we get the boxes open without breaking all our fingernails (the boxes are apparently sealed with the same glue that holds the space shuttle together). Next we get to rip open the dozens of net bags the marbles are packed in. Finally, we lug the boxes around again, spreading out the marbles over the books and the corners of the table. If we have time, we wipe off the resin dust before the doors open on Friday night and the women start coming in—sometimes fifteen to twenty thousand of them! That's when the *real* joy-splashing work begins!

As the women stream by the table, my helpers and I say to those passing near the table, "Would you like a splash of joy?" Then, even though we also hand out little papers that explain the marbles, we have to say approximately 2,887,922 times (or at least it seems that way!), "Put it on your windowsill. When it sparkles it will remind you of all the ways God blesses your life . . . Yes, they're free . . . No, we don't have a different color . . . Yes, you can take one for your sister (friend, mother, daughter, coworker, pastor's wife, or bus driver) too . . . No, it doesn't stick to anything. It's not a magnet."

Then, after a couple of hours of this, our "speech" changes to, "No, I'm sorry. They're all gone . . . No, there's really no way to order them; Barb just has them sent to each conference site, and we give them out there . . . Yes, they're really all gone. I know . . . Just a little while ago we had a whole mountain of them—in fact we had nearly two hundred pounds of them. But they're all gone now."

Believe me, there comes a time during every conference when you don't dare mention the words "splash of joy" around my helpers! They're liable to flash you a look that will frost your face for days! That's why we all laughed until we cried (*really* cried!) when a woman wrote me recently suggesting that we "extend" the splash-of-joy idea by selling *jars* of the marbles to conference attendees. We could call them "jars of joy," she suggested.

Now, I have to admit that her idea is really a good one—from a marketing standpoint. But the mere thought of shipping *jars* and *more* marbles everywhere we go just about sent us all into hysterics. Feeling a little mischievous, I shared the woman's letter with one of the gals who works at my table. She laughed too. And then she cried. And then she said, "Barb, I quit!"

No, the splashes cause us enough problems already. We won't be selling them in jars anytime soon. In fact, by the end of a conference, we have the firm opinion that we don't ever want to hear the phrase "splash of joy" again!

Then we go home, and inevitably the letters arrive . . .

"Dear Barb," one might say, "this has been an awful year

for me. I didn't want to come to the conference, but my friend from church insisted. We stopped by your book table and one of the women there smiled at me and said, 'Do you need a splash of joy?' She held out this little, flat marble and said it would remind me of all my blessings. I dropped it in my pocket and planned to forget about it. But every time I stuck my hand in my pocket, I felt it there. And gradually, the fact hit me: Despite all that has happened to me, I have many blessings to be thankful for. I'm healthy. My husband loves me. I have good friends who care about me. Thanks, Barb, for helping me remember."

The woman who suggested that we sell jars of splashes added that she had come to the Women of Faith conference "feeling anything but joyful." She was involved in a very stressful legal separation from her husband, she said, and her life "felt out of control, frustrating, unfair." Then she picked up "the silly little thing" at my book table.

> I put it in my coat pocket and fingered it all day, and for the few days following. It truly did remind me of God's love for me and kept me looking for those small but precious splashes of joy He is so faithful to inject into every day if we will but look for them, acknowledge them, and receive them. As I drove home from the conference that day, I asked the Lord to help me find some of these "splashes" to share with others as you had done.

She eventually found something similar and started handing them out.

> First, I explained to my husband and children what "splashes of joy" were and gave them each one to keep and one to share. Over the next few days I consistently put "splashes" in my pockets and shared them with others . . . a little boy in my son's first grade class who was discouraged, my doctor, my

dear friend . . . , a lady at the checkout in the grocery store, my babysitter and her daughter, complete strangers whose path I providentially passed. Not one person was anything less than thrilled, blessed, and encouraged.

Finally, my thoughts turned to my mother. . . . She is a widow, must work full-time at a stressful job to make a living, and is frequently prone to being discouraged. . . . I sent her a bag of "splashes," explained the idea to her, and urged her to buy a pretty jar for her desktop to put them in. My children and I made a little sign to put inside the jar that said "splashes of joy." She loved the idea and is now using these splashes, as I am, to encourage others in her environment.

Another letter writer said she gave her sister the little blue splash she picked up at the book table when the Women of Faith tour was in Pittsburgh in September 1996. The sister, a happily married mother and grandmother, was in a battle against breast cancer that would continue another two years. She put the little marble on her stereo, where it often brought a smile to her face.

The sister was in the hospital in November 1998 when the doctors gave her only a few days to live. What happened next was an incredible act of love that grew out of adversity. The woman's letter described it beautifully:

She wanted to die at home. As the doctors and nurses made preparations for her to be discharged a few days later, she made preparations for her funeral.

That's when she remembered the splash of joy. She had her daughter go from store to store until she could find more of those little flat marbles! She bought a bunch of them, all different colors, and filled a deep, clear glass bowl with them. As the doctors and nurses came, changed shifts, etc., she asked them to dip their hands into the bowl and take a splash of joy with them. She had them all in tears by the time she was discharged! But they won't forget her . . . or the joy she infused them with! . . .

She died a few days later at the age of forty-five. At her funeral, bowls full of splashes of joy were placed around the church, and everyone was invited to take some home along with a little paper explaining what they were. All her life, the sister had been allergic to flowers. But for her memorial service the sanctuary was overflowing with flowers "from everyone who never could give her any while she was alive!" the letter continued. "It was everyone's last gesture of love to her. And the splashes of joy were her last gesture of love to those she left behind."

Reading the letter, I was so touched by this woman's beautiful story. Then came the part that made my tears flow:

Barbara, you just have no idea how very much your little idea has turned into a huge thing. Your splashes of joy have been shared all over Steuben County, New York now. Even people who didn't personally know my sister have requested a splash after hearing about the little marbles. I'm sure there are hundreds of stories people from all over could tell about how the splashes of joy have touched their lives.

I apologize for making this such a lengthy letter when all I really wanted to tell you was "thank you" for the joy you share. Hopefully you have been touched yourself by the joy that is now being "boomeranged" back to you!

More than you'll know, Honey . . . more than you'll ever know.

"HEAVEN MUST HAVE SENT YOU"

Too Blest to Be Stressed

From these letters you can understand how these "silly little things" I call splashes of joy are not only boomerang blessings to those of us who hand them out. They're also pebbles in a pond, generating ripples of blessings that radiate in all directions. Certainly, some of them get dropped into purses or pockets and are quickly forgotten. But once in a while, that little piece of polished glass touches a life in a way no one could have expected. And the result is simply awesome.

Being an angel lover, I like to think my coworkers and I (the "splashers") are doing angel work when we toss these little marbles into the sea of ladies who attend the Women of Faith conferences (the "splashees"). In response, we (along with the others they share the idea with) receive the most heartwarming encouragement. As one letter-writer put it, "the splashes of joy become showers of blessing" to *all* of us.

The goodness generated by those colorful little marbles boomerangs back to us. It revs us up and charges our batteries so that we can lug those boxes around and repeat our little speeches another few thousand times a week or so later!

Temporary Assignments

A suspicion of angel activity occurred to me last year when the Women of Faith conference was held in Buffalo, New York. During the afternoon before the event began, Bill and I visited Niagara Falls. (We laughed all the way up there, recalling how I'd told one of the conference workers that Bill and I were taking the afternoon off to "do the Niagara thing" and she'd misunderstood and thought I'd said we were doing the *Viagra* thing, referring to the new drug that had just come out for men.)

What a breathtaking place Niagara Falls is! Riding the little *Maid of the Mist* boat right up to the foot of the majestic falls and feeling the power of the thundering water as it plunges over the precipice, I was spellbound by the extraordinary beauty of this natural wonder. Gazing up at the white curtain of foam, crystals of light seemed to sparkle in the sunlight, and I was suddenly overwhelmed, realizing how the falls symbolize God's outpouring love that refreshes us.

The Niagara Falls story that made me think of angels concerns two children who fell into the river above the falls during a boating accident several years ago. The boat was destroyed, its operator was killed, and a seven-year-old boy was swept over the falls. Miraculously, he survived and was rescued by the *Maid of the Mist.*

His little sister was near the brink of the falls when a New

Jersey tourist spotted her. The tourist climbed over the guard
rail, stepped into the water, and reached out over the mur-
derous current toward the child. At the last possible moment,
the little girl grasped his thumb. But the additional weight
added to his precarious position in the current caused the res-
cuer, himself, to lose his balance and wobble dangerously
close to the precipice. He called for help, and a second tourist,
a man from Pennsylvania, climbed over the guard rail and
helped both the man and child back to shore.

The rescuers were just two "ordinary" men, two tourists.
And it might be that they simply found extra adrenaline that
day to pull the little girl back from plummeting over the falls.
But many who saw them risk their lives for a stranger com-
pared them with angels.[19]

Just as the Bible instructs us to "entertain strangers" because
they might be angels in disguise, we should also be ready to
"rescue strangers" if God decides to use *us* in angelic ways.
Most of us probably hope He won't send us out to lean over
the edge of Niagara Falls and pull someone back from the
brink of death. Instead He might send us to, say, Omaha—
assigned, unknowingly, to the airplane seat next to a broken-
hearted mother or a hard-hearted father. It could be someone
who's trying to run away from God. Perhaps He might plant
us in a crowd where one person, quietly standing up for what's
right, could make all the difference. He might send us to a
hospital or a prison or a nursing home to clasp the hands of
someone there who is desperately reaching out for God.

Boomerang Blessings
Opportunities to do good are everywhere, but they're sometimes fleeting. We move on by and later tell ourselves, *I should
have done this or that.*

There's a wonderful story about how this kind of decision to
do good can boomerang blessings back to us. The tale describes
a king who wanted to know what kind of people inhabited his
kingdom. So he had a huge boulder rolled into the middle of a
major roadway, then he hid among the trees, watching to see

what would happen. A merchant, his wagon piled high with goods, rolled to a stop before the huge boulder. Briefly, he considered moving it but decided it wasn't worth his time or effort. He guided the horses around the rock, creating new ruts in the grass beside the road. Next a coach came along carrying a kingdom dignitary. When the driver stopped, the official stuck his head out the window and impatiently demanded that the driver hurry on around the obstacle. A farmer appeared next, pulling a hay wagon. He, too, detoured around the boulder without trying to remove it.

Finally, a single rider approached. He could easily have ridden around the boulder on his horse. But he stopped, looked around for a tree limb to use as a lever, and managed to pry the stone from its resting place and send it rolling into the ditch. As he started to mount his horse and ride away, he noticed a leather pouch lying in the road where the stone had been. Inside was a hundred gold pieces and a note from the king, explaining that the gold was for the person who took the time to remove the boulder.[20]

That story reminds me of another boomerang blessing that came to us because of something that happened at a Women of Faith conference. We accept only cash and checks at my book table, no credit cards. When women want to buy books and don't have their checkbooks or enough cash, we tell them to take the books and send the cash later. Folks are usually astonished to believe we would trust them this way, but as far as we know, we've never had anyone who took the books and didn't eventually pay.

The special blessing came last summer, when the conference was on the West Coast. We told a woman who had brought only a credit card to take the books she wanted and mail a check later—and she did. The blessing came when the woman went home and told her husband, a non-Christian, how we had trusted her with the books. He was so amazed he told her to send a check to me, not for the amount of the books she bought, but for five hundred dollars to support our work with hurting families!

Of course, there's no guarantee that every good deed we do will result in that person returning the favor. But I'm convinced that, sooner or later, one way or another, a blessing will come. But even if there were no possibility of a boomerang effect, we know by being kind to one another we are doing God's will—and for Christians, that should be blessing enough.

Wherever we go, we should be aware of the possibilities to do the work of angels—not to preach and quote Scripture but to serve and minister to others, even those who can never repay our kindness. Perhaps, in time, they'll pass the blessing on to someone else and not to us.

Whenever we can, we should follow the example of the kind-hearted woman who spotted a little boy, ten years old, standing in front of a New York City shoe store, barefooted, on a cold November day. The woman stopped and asked him, "What are you looking at?"

"I was asking God to give me a pair of those shoes," the little boy replied.

The woman stepped toward the door of the store and held out her hand. "Come with me," she said.

She took a half-dozen pairs of socks off the rack as they walked toward the back of the store. There she asked a clerk to bring her a basin of warm water and a towel. The man quickly complied.

Removing her coat and gloves, the woman knelt down and washed the boy's little feet and dried them with the towel. She eased the socks over his cold toes and then asked the clerk to find him the shoes he'd been eying in the store window. The boy watched in wonder as her requests were fulfilled. Finally the clerk dropped the extra socks in a bag, totaled the bill, and accepted the woman's money.

"You'll be a lot more comfortable now," she told the boy, smiling, as they walked together through the doorway. As she turned to go, the astonished lad caught her hand and looked up in her face.

"Are you God's wife?" he asked.

As Christians we are Christ's bride, His church. When we

do angel work in His name, we demonstrate His love to others. These kindnesses don't have to be daring or costly. An encouraging word—or simply an attitude of joy—can often make all the difference to someone who's given up hope. A little smile can brighten someone's day. And while you're smiling you might as well go one step further and share a chuckle or two. You know what they say: A laugh is just a smile with a sound track.

C. S. Lewis said, "The best argument for Christianity is Christians: their joy, their certainty, their completeness." Lewis also warned, however, that Christians can be "the strongest argument *against* Christianity . . . when they are somber and joyless, when they are self-righteous and smug, . . . when they are narrow and repressive, then Christianity dies a thousand deaths."[21] Let's resolve to be angels of joy and missionaries of mirth wherever we go today—and every day!

Cloud Busters

An angel is someone
who brings out the angel in you.

People with a heart for God
have a heart for people.[22]

Remember:
Each of us can decrease the suffering of the world
by adding to its joy.[23]

Make a friendship kit:

Rubber band: To hold friends close
Tissue: To dry a tear
Recipe: To make and share
Stationery: To write a note of encouragement
Band-aid: A reminder that friends help heal a
          hurting heart
Poem: To express your love
Prayer: To lead your friend to God

We are each of us angels with only one wing.
And we can only fly by embracing each other.

Luciano de Crescenzo

PUT YOUR ARMS AROUND EACH OTHER

> *(This page 1 banner headline appeared in* The
> Tennessean *on April 18, 1998, quoting Mayor
> Phil Bredesen the day after a devastating tor-
> nado ravaged much of East Nashville.)*

Always deal reasonably [with others] and don't be
rude. Consider that the stranger with whom you
are dealing may very well be the visitor sitting
beside you in church next Sunday![24]

When Jesus died on the cross and saved you from
sin, He did so not only to get you into heaven but for
an even more important reason. . . . Jesus saved you
. . . in order to make you into a person who could do
magnificent things for others in His name.[25]

It doesn't take great wisdom to energize a person, but it does take sixty seconds. That's the amount of time it takes to walk over and gently hold someone we love.[26]

On Valentine's Day a wrinkled old man sat on the bus seat holding a bunch of fresh roses. Across the aisle was a young girl whose sad eyes seemed to be locked on the floor—except for moments when she glanced back again and again at the man's flowers.

The time came for the old man to get off. Impulsively he thrust the flowers into the girl's lap. "I can see you love the roses," he explained. "I was taking them to my wife, but I know she would like for you to have them. I'll tell her I gave them to you."

The girl accepted the flowers with a delighted smile then watched the old man get off the bus . . . and walk through the gate of a cemetery.

He who overcomes shall thus be clothed in white garments; and I will not erase his name from the book of life, and I will confess his name before My Father, and before His angels.[27]

"YOU MAKE MY SPIRIT SOAR"

Blow ye the trumpet!
Blow it loud and clear.
Blow it so that everyone can hear.
God's people now listen for the final sound
To leave this world and live on holy ground.[1]

Ain't a Gonna Need
This House No Longer

One night about 1916, Harrison Mayes, a young coal miner, was nearly killed by a runaway coal car deep inside a Kentucky mine. Struggling to survive his terrible injuries, Mayes promised God he would dedicate himself to the Lord's work if his life could be spared. God apparently accepted the offer; the coal miner lived to be eighty-eight years old.

It never occurred to Mayes not to keep his end of the bargain with God, but it took awhile to find his own humble niche in God's kingdom of workers. He couldn't carry a tune in a bucket, so gospel singing was definitely out. He was a failure at preaching too.

Ah, but he could use his hands. Soon he began painting signs with Christian slogans on them. His first printed message was "sin not," which he painted on both sides of the family pig! Next he made wooden crosses, and then, as one writer described his zeal, "like an evangelical Johnny Appleseed, he planted them across the Southeast."

Although he kept his job in the coal mine—in fact, he often

worked double shifts to fund his work as God's messenger—his real focus was on planting his crosses all over the country. In the 1940s he began casting concrete signs in the shape of hearts as well as crosses, and he cut biblical messages into the molds: "Prepare to Meet God," or "Jesus Is Coming Soon," or "Get Right with God." Each sign weighed fourteen hundred pounds.

Mayes, who didn't drive, hired a flatbed truck to haul the signs to sites along America's roadways. Then he dug holes and gently "planted" the signs. By the time he was too old to plant any more of his hearts and crosses, thousands of the sturdy cement monuments were standing along highways in forty-four states.

While his focus was on planting roadside crosses, Mayes also used a more ancient means of carrying God's messages. It's estimated that he tucked little Bible verses and other religious notes into as many as fifty thousand bottles of all shapes and set them bobbing down creeks and rivers all over the country.

His son, interviewed for a newspaper article a few months ago, recalled that his father never sought donations but was nevertheless supported by many miners and their churches. If his father had six dollars, the son said, he gave the family three—and spent the rest on his signs.[2]

Now, you might think Harrison Mayes was a little eccentric. In fact you might question his sanity as he carried out his single-minded campaign to crisscross America with crosses. But you could never doubt his devotion to God.

When he died in 1988, he left no fortune for his family to inherit. He had accumulated no earthly treasures to speak of. He seemed to understand the wisdom that says when you go to heaven the only thing you take with you is what you leave behind. What Harrison Mayes left behind was a legacy of love for the Lord—and several thousand simple roadside markers, directing those who came after him toward salvation. A handful of Mayes's crosses and signs are still standing; perhaps you've seen one of them and been reminded: "Jesus Saves."

Can't you just imagine the stoop-shouldered little coal miner standing humbly before God's mighty throne as the Father reviews his good works? Surely Harrison Mayes will see a twinkle in God's eye and hear Him say, "Well done, my good and faithful servant!"

"THIS WORLD IS NOT MY HOME"

Used by permission of Samuel J. Butcher, creator of Precious Moments.

The Narrow Road to Heaven

Heaven will be a spacious place, and all sorts of treasures will be available to us there. But the entryway is too small for a moving van; we can't take anything with us to paradise except the love we carry inside our hearts. Harrison Mayes knew that lesson well.

Jesus said, "The gate is small and the road is narrow that leads to true life."[3] When we read this verse we usually think of how easily we can stumble off the narrow beam of light that illuminates the route to heaven. But it also reminds us there's a parking area outside the gate and a sign that says, "Wide Loads Exit Here." That's the drop-off area where we lay down all those things that have meant so much to us on earth: the bank deposits, jewelry, lavish homes, and luxury cars. None of it will fit through the narrow way to heaven.

But that's not all we leave in the parking area outside the pearly gates. All our worries are to be dropped off there, too, along with our broken hearts and our tears.

My daughter-in-love Shannon has so beautifully described to me the way she saw one of her and my son Barney's friends "gradually let go of the things of the world and grasp the things of heaven" as he neared the end of a ten-year struggle with cancer. It was a gradual process, she said, and it illustrated to her how people "struggle to come into this life and struggle to go out of it."

As time passed, the friend made a remarkable transition, letting go of the concerns of the world, letting go of the initial anxiety he'd felt when first diagnosed, releasing the frustration that had tormented him, and taking hold of the peace that seemed to flow out of heaven and wrap him securely in God's comfort blanket. Finally, when he died, it was clear he understood that he was taking nothing with him, Shannon said, "nothing except the love of those whose lives he had touched."

The beautiful words of Ecclesiastes teach us there is "a time to get, and a time to lose; a time to keep, and a time to cast away."[4] There are occasions in life when we must hang on— grip the hand of God tightly and struggle fiercely to hold on to His promises. And then, at the end of our lives, there is a time to let go of the struggles and simply fall into those everlasting arms of the Father.

Just think of what America was like when the Europeans first began exploring the New World. On land, they walked or rode horses over nothing more than simple footpaths—routes worn by Indians or wildlife moving single-file through the forests. As more settlers felt the urge to move westward, the single paths became double to accommodate the wheels of the wagons that hauled families and their belongings. When the pioneers left home, they packed their Conestogas with everything from pearls to pianos—the treasures they were certain they would need in their new home.

But something interesting often happened as the days passed and the hardships began. Gradually, the priorities of many of the pioneers changed as their journey continued. Beside a river swollen by flood waters, they might discard the piano that threatened to sink the wagon as they prepared to ford the stream. At the foot of the mountains, many of them abandoned the heirloom chests, trunks, and other furniture that had been handed down for generations. In the middle of the desert, they left behind the wagon and all it contained so that when they emerged on the other side—*if* they emerged—they sometimes had nothing left but their lives. And once again, they needed only a narrow trail, one person wide.

That's kind of like the way we will approach heaven: standing alone, empty-handed, with all our "important" earthly priorities littering the roadway behind us as it narrows down to a path just one person wide. When we stand at the foot of God's throne, we'll have nothing to show for our toil on earth except the life we've lived for Him. That's what folks mean when they say we can't take anything with us to heaven but we can send it on ahead. We do so by investing ourselves and our love for God in the hearts and lives of others.

> As for man, his days are like grass,
> he flourishes like a flower of the field;
> the wind blows over it and it is gone,
> and its place remembers it no more.[5]

While we can take nothing with us to heaven, we can leave a lot of important things behind to encourage our friends and loved ones—and very few of them have anything to do with material goods.

Do Others See God in Us?

All we can take with us to heaven is what we leave behind in the lives we touch. A minister's words at a memorial service also illustrate this kind of legacy: A woman died shortly after moving to the city where her only child, a woman named Cathy, lived, far from the old hometown. Because Cathy was so beloved in her own church, she decided to have her mother's memorial service there, among her own closest friends, instead of back in the hometown she and her mother had shared.

At the service, the minister said, "I didn't know Cathy's mother. But I know Cathy, and I'm sure I saw her mother in her—just as I know I see Jesus in her. Cathy was her mother's child, and she is Jesus' child. And in her life we see the love they both invested in her."

Trust funds can be handed down. Family heirlooms can be passed on. But sooner or later whatever earthly treasures we leave to our loved ones will wind up in that pile of rubble alongside the narrowing pathway to heaven. The only legacy worth anything is our footprints for them to follow . . . right up to God's throne. In the light of eternity, nothing else matters.

When a man was moving to a new town, his friends bought a tiny young sapling, a flowering tree, for him to plant at his new home as a reminder of all the good times they had shared. The man nurtured the tree in the lawn of his new home, and soon it was taller than he was. Each spring its growing array of blossoms lifted his spirits and reminded him of his friends back "home."

But then he had to move again, and this time it was to another part of the country. He couldn't bear to leave the tree behind because it meant so much to him. So he called a tree expert and insisted, "No matter what the expense, I want to take this tree with me."

But the specialist just shook his head. "This tree won't live where you're going," he said. "It can't survive that climate. All you can do is tell the new owners its story and help them understand how special it is."

That's how many of us ended up with the Tree of Life taking root in our hearts. Its seed was a gift from someone else, someone who had nurtured its growth in his own life—and then passed the gift on to us. What a privilege it is to receive such an awesome inheritance! Its value is beyond any earthly comparison. It is Jesus' gift to us of eternal life, something we don't deserve, didn't work for, and can't buy for any price.

The New Me

While it's important to think of the spiritual legacies we leave behind, it's downright fun to think about the inheritances awaiting us in heaven. Imagining myself in God's constant presence, joyfully enveloped in His eternal love, I get really excited. And I can hardly wait to move into my own mansion, walk the streets of gold, and join the heavenly chorus!

But there's something else that makes me positively giddy just to think about. It's the new body I'll have instantly when the rapture is complete. The Bible says, "It will take only a second—as quickly as an eye blinks—when the last trumpet sounds. The trumpet will sound, and those who have died will be raised to live forever, and we will all be changed."[6]

An old, old hymn describes the process so joyfully:

> On that resurrection morning
> When the dead in Christ shall rise
> I'll have a new body, praise the Lord, I'll have
>   a new life.
> Sown in weakness, raised in power, ready to live
>   in paradise,
> I'll have a new body, praise the Lord, I'll have
>   a new life eternal![7]

Now, the Bible doesn't say anywhere that we get to *choose* what kind of new body we get, but just in case we do, I plan to order something in a petite size! For years I've said my body's a perfect ten but I keep it covered with fat so it won't get scratched. Maybe in heaven my "inner" dream body will finally be revealed! If it is, I imagine I'll be cute—like the caricature of me that Word Publishing included in a promotion.

It's fun to pretend we'll be able to pick and choose specific body parts in heaven rather than being assigned a whole new model at once. Let's see . . . I might ask for a dynamic voice like Billy Graham's, a caring heart like Mother Teresa's, and tireless feet like John the Baptist's. Maybe while I'm at it I could request the patience of Job, the artistic ability of Michelangelo, the wisdom of Solomon, the insight of C. S. Lewis, and hands like Noah's—or perhaps hands like the Master Carpenter's . . .

When we get our new bodies and our new, eternal lives in heaven, inevitably there will be some tears among those we leave behind. (At least we hope there will! As someone said, "Parting is such sweet sorrow—unless you can't stand the person!") But any tears that are shed here on earth will simply reflect the light of heaven's joy when we move into our new bodies and our eternal life in heaven begins. Then we'll look back and understand the meaning of the observation that "God's most precious gems are crystallized tears."

Moving Day

Yes, I'm looking forward to moving into that new body God has promised me. No more aches and pains, no more groans, no more corns or calluses. How wonderful to think of moving out of my earthly body that is quickly becoming like the dilapidated house described in the wonderful old song:

> This old house is a gettin' shaky,
> This old house is a gettin' old,
> This old house lets in the rain,
> This old house lets in the cold;
> On my knees I'm a gettin' chilly
> But I feel no fear or pain,
> 'Cause I see an angel peekin' through
> A broken window pane.
>
> Ain't a gonna need this house no longer,
> Ain't a gonna need this house no more;
> Ain't got time to fix the shingles,
> Ain't got time to fix the floor,
> Ain't got time to oil the hinges nor to mend
>   no window pane;
> Ain't a gonna need this house no longer,
> I'm a gettin' ready to meet the saints![8]

The song's grammar isn't exactly exemplary, but the attitude it expresses thrills my heart every time I hear it. Every now and then, I imagine there's an angel peeking through a broken part of my heart, winking at me and nodding his little head, reassuring me that I'm "gettin' ready to meet the saints" up there. Knowing what wonders await me in heaven, I have absolutely no fear of death, because I know . . .

> When they drop these bones down in the ground
> I'll be livin' on the other side.[9]

Just thinking about trading in our worn-out earthly bodies for new models gives me a little boost. As Joni Eareckson Tada says, "This thought alone makes the earthly toil not only bearable, but lighter." Joni compares our new lives in heaven with the way her horse used to feel when the mare was finally headed home:

> I can remember how, after hours of riding my horse to check gates and fences, my weary mount would be wet with sweat, her head hanging low. I had to urge her to put one tired hoof in front of another. Then as soon as she caught a whiff of home or recognized the fences of her own pasture, her ears would pick up and her pace would quicken. The nearer we came to the barn, the more eager her trot. After a quick unsaddling, she would joyfully roll in the dirt and take long, deep drinks from the trough. How good it feels for a beast to be home, to be able to rest.
> How good it will feel for us to rest, to be at home.[10]

Guaranteed a Winner
For Christians, no matter what happens to us here, we're gonna come out winners on the other side! As someone said:

> God believes in me, so my situation is never hopeless.
> He walks beside me, so I am never alone.
> God is on my side, so I can never lose.

That promise really came alive for me last year because of something that happened at a Women of Faith conference on the East Coast. When it was my turn to speak to the sixteen thousand women attending the conference, I showed a little button that says, "Someone Jesus loves has AIDS."

The button is really a corollary to another succinct idea that's become a nationwide trend—the initials "WWJD?" that adorn everything from jewelry to license plates, asking "What would Jesus do?" Tying together the two ideas, I asked the audience, "What would Jesus do?" when it came to dealing with those who might be considered outcasts, especially homosexuals and others afflicted by HIV and AIDS. Of course the answer was that He would love them.

It is so easy to glibly *say* that we apply the "WWJD?" principle to our lives. Maybe we point to the time we spend volunteering in the church nursery. Or maybe we let someone cut in front of us in rush-hour traffic, or we drop a dollar in the Salvation Army's red bucket at Christmastime. It might even be possible to get a little smug, thinking we're doing what Jesus would do. But what about those situations that aren't so pristine and noble? What about our dealings with those down-and-out people who are outside the mainstream? That's the issue that arose for several of us at the recent conference.

Right after I had spoken and had shown the AIDS button and talked about "WWJD?" being the guideline for all of life, I was hustled down to the speakers' lunchroom to grab a bite to eat. Suddenly our darling conference director, Christie Barnes, came bounding into the room, her beautiful brown eyes as big as saucers. She blurted out that a woman was upstairs on the main concourse threatening suicide unless she got help! The suicidal woman, Toni, was a prostitute in that city, Christie explained, and she also had full-blown AIDS. Toni was afraid that her pimp, who had already shot and cut her previously when she had tried to leave him, was trying to find her.

Evidently Toni had slept in a dumpster the night before and had walked a couple of miles to get to the conference. A nice, well-dressed woman outside the coliseum had befriended her and another woman gave her a ticket to get in to hear the program.

After she heard me speak about "WWJD?" and loving those with AIDS, Toni became agitated, insisting on seeing me. When she learned that I wouldn't be coming back up to my book table because we'd sold out, she started loudly insisting that she *had* to see me. Women of Faith staff members on the concourse tried to talk with her, but Toni would have none of it. She began raising a ruckus and threatening suicide.

The coliseum's security force responded, counselors at the New Life Clinics table made themselves available, and the city police were summoned. Yet with all the professional people who COULD help, the woman was apparently determined to talk to ME, of all people! Eventually a staff member contacted Christie, who scurried to relay the woman's demands.

Quickly I gathered some other Women of Faith workers plus my own helper, and we dashed into one of the coliseum's locker rooms where Christie had led the tall, unkempt, slovenly dressed woman. She was about thirty-five years old, wearing ill-fitting shorts, a dirty T-shirt, and a baseball cap. We settled onto a couch in the lounge area, and I asked Toni to tell us what was wrong. It took awhile for her to settle down, but eventually the story came pouring out about her hard life as a prostitute and her desperate need to escape from her violent pimp. She was sure if he found her he would kill her. Then she pulled up her pant leg and showed us the bullet wound where he had shot her once before. It was a hole about the size of a plum; it looked like a small funnel that had been embedded in her thigh. Then she showed us a scar along the side of her face, the result of his recent knife attack.

Knowing she had full-blown AIDS, I looked around at the other women, who were listening in horror to her story. During the twenty years I've been involved with Spatula Ministries, I've had plenty of contact with AIDS victims, and I've met people with some incredibly brutal stories. But I suspected that none of those other women had even talked with a prostitute before, let alone one with AIDS. Seeing their faces touched by gentle compassion and watching as they repeatedly reached out to hug the trembling woman, I was amazed to see what was happening to them.

Toni said she desperately wanted to get out of her life of prostitution. She wanted to become a Christian, but she had to get away from her pimp. She hoped to make it to Chicago where she had family to shelter her and she would be safe.

When she'd finished her story, I offered my most encouraging smile and gave her the little button I'd shown during my talk, the one that said, "Someone Jesus loves has AIDS." With shaky hands, she fastened it to her dirty T-shirt, and we began to talk about how she could come out of that life. We reminded her that Jesus loved her and that she could have a new heart and a new life. She obviously grasped these ideas wholeheartedly, and right then and there she prayed with us to accept Christ as her Savior. We all jubilantly joined her in saying a loud "Amen!"

But there was more work to be done, and it had to be done quickly. Toni was smelly and dirty, having slept in the dumpster the night before. So a shower was top priority. The other women rushed out to find the things she would need. One of the gals hurried off to find soap, shampoo, and towels and to collect enough money to buy her a bus ticket to Chicago. Another rushed up to the concourse to get some clothes from the conference venders—T-shirt, chambray shirt, sweatshirt, and anything else that would fit a medium size.

Meanwhile, I took her into the shower room to get started

on the cleanup mission. My old Baptist habits came out while we were in the shower, and for a moment I thought perhaps I could baptize her right there. But things were just too crazy, with water flying everywhere from about fifty shower jets protruding from a big pole in the center of the room.

As Toni stepped into the shower, I saw a huge, gaping wound that ran from her neck down under her breast to her sternum; it looked fresh and untreated. "You really need to have a doctor look at that," I told her, but she protested, saying if she didn't get out of the city, she would have more injuries than just a knife wound. After that she sat quietly on a little stool while I shampooed her hair and helped her scrub down.

Now, I have to insert a personal note here. Bill and I had been away from home two weeks when this conference began, and when I left home I knew I probably wouldn't have a chance to have my hair done. So I had brought along a wig, just in case of an "emergency." When I had looked in the mirror that morning, I'd decided this was an EMERGENCY day (little did I know!). So there I was in the shower room with Toni, wearing my wig and darting in and out of the squirting water. And do you know what a wig does when you wear it in a shower room with hot water shooting down on it? Well, it shrinks up into little frizzy sausages! But at the time I didn't even notice, because I was so intent on getting Toni scrubbed clean and headed out on her new life.

In a few moments the other gals came running back with all the necessities—clothes, a hairbrush, and enough money to buy the bus ticket. Before long, Toni had clean hair, a clean body, and clean clothes emblazoned with "Women of Faith." Then we gathered around her again, our arms entwined around each other's shoulders, and prayed. We asked God to give Toni a clean heart. "Thank you, dear Lord, for giving *all* of us a fresh start and a new beginning each and every day," we prayed. "And thank you for bringing Toni to us so we could share in the fresh start she's beginning in You right now."

At that moment, the (former) prostitute was in a win-win situation. If she escaped and got on the bus and rejoined her family in Chicago, she had a brand-new start, a forgiven past, and a new life to serve the Lord. She could know that God could no longer see her sin, because He had removed it "as far as the east is from the west." She could begin a new life in a bright, clean future.

But if the pimp caught her again—and even if he killed her, as she feared—she would be *safe in the arms of Jesus.* From that moment on, her life was hidden in Christ. If she died, she would go immediately into the presence of God as her new faith in Christ transported her into heaven for eternal life. EITHER WAY SHE WAS A WINNER!

"If you get to heaven before I do," I told her with a smile, "you start polishing up those pearly gates, because I'll be coming too before long."

Then it was time to go. We all started for the door, but Toni suddenly stopped, her eyes wide. "My pin!" she said, patting her chest where the AIDS button had been attached to her old T-shirt. She ran over to the trash can and pulled the pin off the old, dirty shirt we had discarded when she got into the shower. She smiled through her tears as she fastened it to her new Women of Faith blouse, and we all hugged her one more time.

We walked her through the little crowd of people who had gathered outside the locker room—the security guards, counselors, and Women of Faith workers who were waiting to see what would happen. The police officer who had been summoned when the suicide threat was made was still waiting too. He had told one of the workers that he had arrested the woman before for prostitution and knew she had had "trouble with her pimp." We assumed he thought we were pretty foolish for scurrying around so excitedly to assist this poor, degenerate woman.

A taxi had been called, and we helped Toni limp across the coliseum plaza and climb into the seat, instructing the driver to take her directly to the bus depot. Then the cab pulled away, and we waved her off, overwhelmed by the transformation that had taken place right before our eyes: clean body, clean clothes, clean heart, NEW WOMAN!

All this had taken some time, and I had to hurry back up on the platform to join the other speakers saying our final good-bye to the women at the conference. It was then that I realized what had happened to my "hair." It was quite a sight to behold, I'm sure—half of my wig fluffy and full and the other side shrunk up into tight, fuzzy little sausage curls.

The program ended, and we filed out through an exit reserved for the speakers. The same police officer was standing there. As I walked past him, he put his arm out as if to stop me, and I thought, *Oh no! Now what?* But his words were so special. He leaned down and said into my ear, his voice raised so I could hear him above the loud music, "Thank you for what you did for that woman. You probably saved her life."

His words came as such a surprise, because we had assumed he thought we were silly to try and help her. And here he was, as touched by the whole thing as we were!

We may never know the final outcome of this story. We don't know if Toni made it to Chicago or if she was killed by her pimp. God only gives the final score when the game is over. And for Toni the game *isn't* over. But we DO know that the lives of the other women who were in that locker room, exhibiting the "WWJD?" message, were changed that day. None of the other women had ever had the opportunity to embrace such a down-and-out person, a woman with AIDS who came out of a dumpster to touch their lives. Some of them may not even have known what a pimp is, and they had certainly never embraced a prostitute! But there they were, ministering to her with love and concern, praying for her, hugging her, and sending her off with great sympathy for her needs.

When God can take a broken, fractured life and transform it through others who are doing what Jesus would do . . . that is the real test of "WWJD?" I know it changed things in MY life, and all those other helping women experienced a change as well. They appreciated the opportunity to really DO something Jesus would do for that wounded, hurting soul.

Only God knows the final result. Deuteronomy 29:29 says, "The secret things belong to the LORD." We may not know the full story until we get to heaven. The whole thing could have been a scam, just a way to take advantage of others' kind hearts. But I firmly believe that no matter what happens to Toni, God has already used the experience for something good. The impression that incident made on those darling helpers at the Women of Faith conference—as well as many of those who were gathered outside the locker-room door—will last a lifetime. They've had a real taste now of doing what Jesus would do under stressful conditions—and they will never be the same.

Ready to Go!

The experience with the prostitute also reinforced in us the fact that as Christians, we're ready for *anything!* If life serves us up a challenge we cannot overcome here on earth—we still come out on top in heaven! We win, no matter what! That's the gift we shared with Toni in the locker room: the assurance that victory is hers, no matter who (or *what*) wins the race down here in the cesspools of life. The secret is to be ready. For years, I've treasured a poem that carries just that warning. It's appeared in a previous book, and I wanted to include it for you one more time in this volume that's focused on being ready for the Lord's return:

'Twas the night before Jesus came and all through
     the house
Not a creature was praying, not one in the house.
Their Bibles were lain on the shelf without care
In hopes that Jesus would not come there.

The children were dressing to crawl into bed,
Not once ever kneeling or bowing a head.
And Mom in her rocker with the babe on her lap
Was watching the Late Show while I took a nap.

When out of the east there arose such a clatter,
I sprang to my feet to see what was the matter.

Away to the window I flew like a flash
Tore open the shutters and threw up the sash!

When what to my wondering eyes should appear
But angels proclaiming that Jesus was here!
With a light like the sun sending forth a bright ray
I knew in a moment this must be THE DAY!

The light of His face made me cover my head
It was Jesus! Returning just like He said.
And though I possessed worldly wisdom
        and wealth,
I cried when I saw Him in spite of myself.

In the Book of Life, which He held in His hand,
Was written the name of every saved man.
He spoke not a word as He searched for my name;
When He said, "It's not here," my head hung
        in shame.

The people whose names had been written
        with love
He gathered to take to His Father above.
With those who were ready He arose without
        a sound
While all the rest were left standing around.

I fell to my knees, but it was too late;
I had waited too long and thus sealed my fate.
I stood and I cried as they rose out of sight;
Oh, if only I had been ready tonight!

In the words of this poem the meaning is clear;
The coming of Jesus is drawing near.
There's only one life, and when comes the
        last call
We'll find that the Bible was true after all![11]

The Second Coming

To the warning of the poem, these ancient words from the Book of Revelation echo a loud "Amen!"

> Look, he is coming with the clouds, and every eye will see him, even those who pierced him; and all the peoples of the earth will mourn because of him. So shall it be! Amen.[12]

When Jesus comes again, every person on earth will see "the Son of Man coming on the clouds of the sky, with power and great glory. And he will send his angels with a loud trumpet call, and they will gather his elect from the four winds, from one end of the heavens to the other."[13] As Charles Wesley's lyrics so vividly describe the scene:

> Lo! He comes, with clouds descending,
> Once for our salvation slain;
> Thousand thousand saints attending, swell
>   the triumph of His train;
> Alleluia! Alleluia! God appears on earth to
>   reign. . . .
>
> Yea, Amen! Let all adore Thee
> High on Thine eternal throne;
> Savior, take the pow'r and glory,
> Claim the kingdom for Thine own.
> O come quickly, O come quickly!
> Alleluia! Come, Lord, come!

Don't you love those last lines? Sometimes when I'm humming that beautiful tune, I add my own little petition: *Come quickly, Lord! It's not that I haven't enjoyed this life You've given me. Oh, I have! Despite all the hard times, the bumps in the road, and the times I've been splattered on the ceiling, I've enjoyed it all, and I've tried to wring every bit of joy out of it that I could. I'm thankful, Lord, but I'm ready. I'm keeping my spiritual ears tuned to the heavenly frequency, so that as soon as I hear those first notes from Your mighty trumpet, I'll be on my way.*

Meet Me at Heaven's Gates
The Lord is coming soon. And there's a part of me that wants to hurry and be first in line at heaven's gates. But there's another part of me that wants to cherish every moment of that transition from earth to heaven. Sometimes I think I'll shoot up to heaven like a rocket, and other times I hope I can float up gently, like steam rising toward the sun. Ruth Bell Graham expressed those feelings so beautifully in one of her poems that I've asked her permission to use it to close out this book. Read the words slowly and let the awesome image form in your mind . . .

> And when I die
> I hope my soul ascends
> slowly, so that I
> may watch the earth receding
> out of sight,
> its vastness growing smaller
> as I rise,
> savoring its recession
> with delight.
> Anticipating joy
> is itself a joy.
> And joy unspeakable
> and full of glory
> needs more
> than "in the twinkling of an eye,"*
> more than "in a moment."
> Lord, who am I
> to disagree?
> It's only we
> have much
> to leave behind;
> so much . . . Before.

These moments
of transition
will, for me, be
time
to adore.[14]

*1 Corinthians 15:52

How eagerly I'm anticipating the "unspeakable joy" of heaven! How about you? Are you ready for that trumpet to sound? Surely it won't be long now! As one friend told me, "I'll see you here, there, or in the air!"

Someday soon, *He's gonna toot, and I'm gonna scoot right outta here!*

Acknowledgments

Many thanks for the jokes, poems, song lyrics, and zany "splashes of joy" in this volume that have been shared by other writers and friends. We have made diligent effort to identify all the original sources, but sometimes this is an impossible task. Other times, our research turned up multiple sources for the same item. Many jokes and stories were found in collections such as *The Best of Bits & Pieces*, and *More of the Best of Bits & Pieces*, both published by Economics Press, Fairfield, New Jersey, and *The Speaker's Quote Book* from Kregel Publishing, Grand Rapids, Michigan. Whenever the source of an unattributed item in this book can be *positively* identified, please contact Word Publishing, P.O. Box 141000, Nashville, TN 37214, so that proper credit can be given in future printings.

Grateful acknowledgment is also given for:

"Hallelujah Square," © 1969 by Ray Overholt Music. Used by permission.

"How Great Thou Art," © 1953 S. K. Hine. Assigned to Manna Music, Inc., 35255 Brooten Road, Pacific City, OR 97135. Renewed 1981. All rights reserved. Used by permission (ASCAP).

"If You Could See Me Now," © 1992 Integrity's Praise! Music/BMI. All rights reserved. Used by permission.

"I'll Fly Away," © 1932 in *Wonderful Message* by Hartford Music Co. Renewed 1960 by Albert E. Brumley & Sons/ SESAC (administered by ICG). All rights reserved. Used by permission.

Notes

Dedication Page

Sam Butcher's additions to the Precious Moments illustration of "This World Is Not My Home" are the trumpet (how appropriate for a book titled *He's Gonna Toot, and I'm Gonna Scoot*) and the boomerang labeled with my motto: *Joy*. Sam knows I'm a believer in the principle of boomerang blessings. In this book, he's helping me toss out a boomerang of love and joy to you!

Chapter 1. We've Got a One-Way Ticket to Paradise!

1. Albert E. Brumley, "I'll Fly Away," © 1932 in *Wonderful Message* by Hartford Music Co. Renewed 1960 by Albert E. Brumley & Sons/SESAC (administered by ICG). All rights reserved. Used by permission.

2. Herbert Buffum, "I'm Going Higher Someday," arr. Alfred B. Smith. Copyright © 1981 by Alfred B. Smith. All rights reserved. Used by permission.

3. Oswald Chambers, *My Utmost for His Highest* (Grand Rapids: Discovery House, 1935), July 29.

4. Matthew 24:30, Revelation 1:7 (KJV), emphasis added.

5. Chambers, ibid.

6. Joni Eareckson Tada, *Heaven . . . Your Real Home* (Grand Rapids: Zondervan, 1995), 198.

7. H. L. Turner, "Christ Returneth."

8. 1 Thessalonians 4:16–17.

9. Charles Ryrie in *Ten Reasons Why Jesus Is Coming Soon: Christian Leaders Share Their Insights*, comp. John Van Diest (Sisters, Ore.: Multnomah, 1998), 190.

10. Tim LaHaye and Jerry Jenkins, *Left Behind* (Wheaton, Ill.: Tyndale, 1995), 16.

11. Joni Eareckson Tada, quoted in *A Place Called Heaven*, comp. Catherine L. Davis (Colorado Springs: Chariot Victor, 1997).

12. Psalm 71:14, emphasis added.

13. Kay Hively and Albert E. Brumley Jr., *I'll Fly Away* (Branson, Mo.: Mountaineer Books, 1990), 134.

14. Psalm 90:10 (RSV), emphasis added.

15. *St. Petersburg* (Fla.) *Times*, 7 September 1998, 10.

16. Dion De Marbelle, "When They Ring Those Golden Bells."

17. Someone sent me this quote from Randy Alcorn's sermon "What Does the Bible Say About Heaven?" posted on his Internet web site.

18. Peggy Andersen, "Seattle company taking rocket-ship reservations," Associated Press article in an undated clipping from the *Orange County Register*.

19. Adapted from *The Best of Bits & Pieces*, comp. Arthur F. Lenehan (Fairfield, N.J.: Economics Press, 1994), 16.

20. Clifford Pugh, *Houston Chronicle*, "Patience wears thin in today's on-the-go society," published 9 July 1997, in the *Denver Post*.

21. Frederick Buechner, *Whistling in the Dark*, quoted in *The Answer to Happiness, Health, and Fulfillment in Life: The Holy Bible Translated for Our Time* with *Selected Writings by Leading Inspirational Authors (The Answer Bible)* (Dallas: Word, 1993).

22. Billy Graham, *Storm Warning* (Dallas: Word, 1992), 312.

23. Stuart K. Hine, "How Great Thou Art!" Copyright 1953 S. K. Hine. Assigned to Manna Music, Inc., 35255 Brooten Road, Pacific City, OR 97135. Renewed 1981. All rights reserved. Used by permission. (ASCAP)

24. Adapted from *Reader's Digest*, June 1998.

25. *The Last Word: Tombstone Wit and Wisdom,* comp. Nicola Gillies (Oxford, England: Dove Tail Books, 1997).

26. *Prairie Home Companion's Pretty Good Joke Book,* vol. 3 (St. Paul: Minnesota Public Radio, 1998), 5.

27. Ibid., 7.

28. "The Good, Clean Funnies List," P.O. Box 12021, Huntsville, Alabama 35815.

29. *More of the Best of Bits & Pieces,* comp. Rob Gilbert, Ph.D. (Fairfield, N.J.: Economics Press, 1997), 40.

30. Psalm 55:6.

Chapter 2. Transposed by Music

1. W. O. Cushing, Ira D. Sankey, "Under His Wings."

2. Mrs. Will L. Murphy, "Constantly Abiding."

3. Kim Noblitt, "If You Could See Me Now," © 1992 Integrity's Praise! Music/BMI. All rights reserved. Used by permission.

4. Robin Hinch, "Giesela Lenhart went 'home' while praising God," *Orange County Register,* 21 March 1998, Metro-6.

5. Johnson Oatman and John R. Sweeney, "Holy, Holy Is What the Angels Sing."

6. Al Smith, *Treasury of Hymn Histories,* published in 1982 by Praise Resources, 2200 Wade Hampton Blvd., Greenville, SC 29615.

7. Kenneth Osbeck, *Amazing Grace* (Grand Rapids: Kregel, 1990), 47.

8. Martin Luther, *What Luther Says,* quoted in *The Answer Bible.*

9. Smith, *Treasury of Hymn Histories.*

10. Source unknown.

11. Adapted from a story by Kirsten Jackson in *Christianity Today.* Date unknown.

12. Source unknown.

13. 1 Chronicles 16:32–33.

Chapter 3. May the Joybells of Heaven Ding-Dong in Your Heart Today

1. W. O. Cushing, "Ring the Bells of Heaven."

2. See Exodus 28:33, 39:25, and Zechariah 14:20.

3. Kenneth W. Osbeck, *101 Hymn Stories* (Grand Rapids: Kregel, 1982), 76–77.

4. "Salvation Army gets $80 million from Kroc," *Orange County Register*, September 1998.

5. Joyce Landorf, *Mourning Song* (Grand Rapids: Baker, 1974), 52–53.

6. Joey O'Connor, *Heaven's Not a Crying Place: Teaching Your Child about Funerals, Death, and the Life Beyond* (Grand Rapids: Revell, 1997), quoted in *Focus on the Family* magazine, August 1998, 7.

7. Genesis 19:27; Exodus 16:7, 34:4; 2 Samuel 23:3–4; Job 1:5; Psalm 5:3; and Isaiah 26:9.

8. Mark 1:35 and Luke 21:38.

9. Adapted from Peter Marshall's story retold by Jeanne Hendricks in *A Place Called Heaven*, comp. Catherine L. Davis (Colorado Springs: Chariot Victor, 1997), 70.

10. Proverbs 25:2 and Deuteronomy 29:29.

11. This epitaph utilizing a portion of Philippians 1:23 (KJV) is quoted in Gillies, *The Last Word*, 25.

12. *The Best of Bits & Pieces*, 130.

13. Dion De Marbelle, "When They Ring Those Golden Bells."

14. Psalm 81:8.

Chapter 4. Stick a Geranium in Your Starry Crown

1. E. E. Hewitt and John R. Sweeney, "I Am Thinking Today."

2. Philippians 4:12–13.

3. 1 Corinthians 9:25.

4. 2 Timothy 4:7–8.

5. James 1:12.

6. 1 Peter 5:4.

7. 1 Thessalonians 2:19 (NKJV).

8. 1 Corinthians 9:24–25.

9. 1 Peter 5:6 (KJV) and John 21:15.

10. Dennis Prager, "A Simple Truth about Happiness," *Reader's Digest*, June 1998, 99.

11. Henri Nouwen, *Here and Now* (New York: Crossroad, 1994, 1997), 28.

12. Ibid., 28–29.

13. Ibid., 29.

14. Revelation 12:1.

15. Norman Vincent Peale, quoted in "Quips, Quotes, Quibbles, & Bits," *Tampa Tribune*, 2 June 1998.

16. Matthew 5:16.

17. Adapted from Stephen Cassettari, *Pebbles on the Road* (New York: HarperCollins/Angus & Robertson, 1993), reprinted in *Bits & Pieces*.

18. *More of the Best of Bits & Pieces*, 33–34.

19. Nouwen, 31.

20. 1 John 4:15–17.

21. Psalm 149:4.

22. Roy Zuck, ed., *The Speaker's Quote Book* (Grand Rapids: Kregel, 1997), 340.

23. Tony Campolo, quoted in *From A to Z Sparkling Illustrations*, comp. Graurorger & Mercer (Grand Rapids: Baker, 1997), 114.

24. *The Best of Bits & Pieces*, 103.

25. Proverbs 14:24.

Chapter 5. Finally, *Fabulously* Home!

1. "Mansion Over the Hilltop," copyright 1949, Singspiration Music (administered by Brentwood-Benson Music Publishing, Inc.). All rights reserved. Used by permission.

2. Ray Overholt, "Hallelujah Square," copyright 1969 by Ray Overholt Music. Used by permission.

3. Adapted from *Chapel Bells* magazine, Fall 98, 6–7.

4. "Even the Lumber Carries Words of Love," *Episcopal Life*, June 1998.

5. Someone told me about this story in an interview with Reeve Lindbergh on Morning Edition, National Public Radio, 21 October 1998, discussing her book, *Under a Wing* (New York: Simon & Schuster, 1998).

6. Augustus Montague Toplady, "Rock of Ages."

7. The photo accompanied a report by Region 9 CBA board member Karen Grosse in *CBA Marketplace*, August 1997, 26. It is used here with the permission of Karen and Ron Grosse.

8. Matthew 11:28 (KJV).

9. Associated Press photo, *Baton Rouge* (La.) *Advocate*, 20 February 1998, 18A.

10. Margaret Guenther, "God's Plan Surpasses Our Best Imaginings," *Episcopal Life*, July/August 1993, 20.

11. This story, originally told by Al Smith, is used here with his permission.

12. *The Christian*, quoted in Zuck, *The Speaker's Quote Book*.

13. *Parables, Etc.*, quoted in Zuck, *The Speaker's Quote Book*.

14. "Un-Real Estate" in the "Off the Wall" column, *San Juan* (New Mexico) *Sun*, 2–8 July 1997.

15. John 14:1–3 (KJV).

Chapter 6. Angels Watchin' Over Me

1. Johnson Oatman and John R. Sweeney, "Holy, Holy Is What the Angels Sing."

2. Billy Graham's statements come from a transcript of CNN's 26 October 1998 broadcast of *Larry King Live*.

3. Luke 16:22.

4. Matthew 24:30–31.

5. Brian Sibley, *C. S. Lewis Through the Shadowlands* (Grand Rapids: Revell, 1985, 1994), 154.

6. Martha McCrackin, quoted in Zuck, *The Speaker's Quote Book.*

7. Revelation 5:11.

8. "The Doctrine of Angels," in Dr. H. L. Willmington, *Willmington's Guide to the Bible* (Wheaton, Ill.: Tyndale, 1981), 776. Scriptures cited include Job 38:7; Psalm 148:1–3; Revelation 9:1–2; 12:3, 4, 7–9.

9. George Howe Colt, "In Search of Angels," *Life* magazine, December 1993, 65.

10. Genesis 3:24.

11. Tada, 66–67.

12. Ibid., 54–55.

13. Ibid., 70.

14. Hebrews 13:1–2.

15. Hebrews 1:14.

16. Billy Graham, *Angels: God's Secret Agents* (Dallas: Word, 1975, 1986, 1994, 1995), 37.

17. Psalm 34:7.

18. Millard and Linda Fuller, *The Excitement Is Building* (Dallas: Word, 1990), 85–86.

19. Based on information in Joan Colgan Stortz, *Niagara Falls* (Markham, Ontario: Irving Weisdorf & Co., 1994, 1995, 1998), 28.

20. Adapted from *Bits & Pieces,* a publication of Economics Press, 6 November 1997, 24.

21. Quoted in Sheldon Vanauken, *A Severe Mercy.*

22. *Our Daily Bread,* 17 June 1998.

23. *Random Acts of Kindness,* intro. by Dawna Markova (New York: Fine Communication, 1997).

24. Mary Hunt, *The Financially Confident Woman* (Nashville: Broadman & Holman, 1996), 170.

25. Tony Campolo, *It's Friday, but Sunday's Comin'* (Dallas: Word, 1993), 88.

26. Gary Smalley with John Trent, *Love Is a Decision* (Dallas: Word, 1996), 70.

27. Revelation 3:5 (NASB).

Chapter 7. Ain't a Gonna Need This House No Longer

1. Charles Wesley, "Blow Ye the Trumpet."

2. This story comes from information in a Scripps Howard News Service article by Fred Brown, "The Way of the Cross," *Cape Coral* (Fla.) *Breeze*, 4 November 1998, 8.

3. Matthew 7:14 (NCV).

4. Ecclesiastes 3:6 (KJV).

5. Psalm 103:15–16.

6. 1 Corinthians 15:51–52 (NCV).

7. "I'll Have a New Life," copyright 1940 Stamps/Baxter Music (administered by Brentwood-Benson Music, Inc.). All rights reserved. Used by permission.

8. Stuart Hamblen, "This Ole House" © 1954 Hamblen Music, renewed 1982. Used by permission. Music available from Hamblen Music, Box 1937, Canyon Country, CA 91386.

9. Rich Cook, "Buried Alive." Used by permission.

10. Tada, 203.

11. "'Twas the Night Before Jesus Came," © 1985 Bethany Farms, Inc. Used by permission of Jeffrey Cummings, Bethany Farms, Inc., St. Charles, Missouri.

12. Revelation 1:7.

13. Matthew 24:30–31.

14. Ruth Bell Graham, *Sitting by My Laughing Fire* (Waco, Tex.: Word, 1977). Used by permission.

More Humor and Inspiration from Everyone's Favorite Geranium Lady

Living Somewhere Between Estrogen and Death
0-8499-3653-5 ✦ Trade Paper ✦ $10.99
0-8499-6270-6 ✦ Audio ✦ $10.99
0-8499-3727-2 ✦ Large Print ✦ $14.99

For women only, this is Barbara Johnson's most unique book in years. With her zany collection of observations about "life between the Blue Lagoon and Golden Pond"—Barbara jumps right in, showing women how to survive growing older with courage and joy.

I'm So Glad You Told Me What I Didn't Wanna Hear
0-8499-3654-3 ✦ Trade Paper ✦ $10.99
0-8499-6218-8 ✦ Audio ✦ $10.99

Bad news about your children carries a triple whammy of pain, worry and "where did we go wrong!" Drawing on her personal experience and the letters she has received from hundreds of hurting people, Barbara Johnson shares hope and humor to encourage parents in seemingly hopeless situations.

Mama Get The Hammer! There's A Fly On Papa's Head
0-8499-3417-6 ◆ Trade Paper ◆ $10.99
0-8499-6192-0 ◆ Audio ◆ $10.99
Barbara Johnson insists that laughing in the face of adversity is not a form of denial, but a proven tool for managing stress, coping with pain, and maintaining hope. She zeroes directly in on the spiritual benefit of a smile, a giggle, and a good, old-fashioned belly laugh.

Pack Up Your Gloomees in a Great Big Box, Then Sit On The Lid and Laugh
0-8499-3364-1 ◆ Trade Paper ◆ $10.99
0-8499-6077-0 ◆ Audio ◆ $10.99
Pack Up Your Gloomees is filled with bittersweet stories of Barbara's journey through the minefields of life, and her wise and encouraging responses to letters from hurting parents. Each chapter ends with a laughter-packed Gloomee Buster.

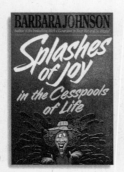

Splashes of Joy in the Cesspools of Life
0-8499-3313-7 ◆ Trade Paper ◆ $10.99
0-8499-6051-7 ◆ Audio ◆ $10.99
0-8499-3941-0 ◆ Large Print ◆ $14.99
Barbara Johnson's approach to life is positive, uplifting, and fun. *Splashes of Joy* offers an invigorating spurt of encouragement and a gentle reminder to splash joy into the lives of others.

Stick A Geranium in Your Hat and Be Happy!

0-8499-3201-7 ♦ Trade Paper ♦ $10.99

0-8499-1260-1 ♦ Audio ♦ $10.99

0-8499-3683-7 ♦ Large Print ♦ $14.99

This is the book that started it all! A survivor of four devastating experiences that equip her with the credentials to help others work through their own pain, Barbara Johnson discovers hope in the hurt and shows while pain is inevitable, misery is optional.

Now Kids and Grandkids Can Experience the Geranium Lady

How do you explain concepts like God's love or true joy to kids? In Barbara Johnson's fun new children's series, kids will laugh as they learn about these truths through the Geranium Lady's zany adventures.

The Upside-Down Frown and Splashes of Joy

0-8499-5844-X ♦ Hard Cover ♦ $7.99

The Geranium Lady and her young friend learn the real secret to turning frowns upside down into smiles. Includes a special Make Your Own "Splashes of Joy!" section.

Super-Scrumptious Jelly Donuts Sprinkled with Hugs

0-8499-5848-2 ♦ Hard Cover ♦ $7.99

In this book, the Geranium Lady introduces kids to hugs through a fun contest. After much laughter and fun, everyone learns that God invented hugs as a way for people to show they care. Includes simple instructions for children to make their very own HUG coupons.

This book has been enjoyed by and shared with:

_____

_____

_____

_____

_____

_____

_____

_____

_____

_____

_____

_____